Know Thy Selfie

Tips, Tricks & Tools for an Awesome Life

By

Iuri Tiago Melo

Interior formatting by access ideas

ISBN: 9781790464784

Table of Contents

Awesome Advice if You Are a Believer   217

To my children, Aydia, Elle, Jona, Kole,
& Leila, who constantly put up with my nonsense
and silliness. May you wake up every morning of
every day with the absolute assurance that your
father loves you and is cheering for you.

To my beloved Katie, The most sincere expression
of how much your love, patience, and friendship
impacts me on a daily basis, is peace.
Thank you 'meu amor'.

To Jed, "it must be nice, it must be nice,
to have [Jed] on your side."
I'm forever indebted. Your wisdom
makes my foolishness readable.
Thank you for your selfless gift.

To the many youth who were brave enough
to step into my office and share their wisdom,
experience, and contagious energy with me.
You inspire me!
Thank you.

Author's Note

This life is absolute genius! It is so completely filled with simplicity and complexity. Life, you'll find, is the complete spectrum. The highs, lows, and valleys in between, are what make living exciting, abundantly rich, and ripe for discovery and experimentation. Don't waste your shot!

This life is for you! It hasn't passed you by. Regardless of where you came from, and despite the ridiculous and scandalous stuff you've already done, greatness lies ahead of you, and within you. **Your problems don't scare me! Your mistakes don't offend me!** Your circumstances don't rob me of the precious hope I have for you and your future. I'm sure you're a disaster—I'm 43 and half the time I still feel like a chicken with its head cut off! But look, there are some things that I absolutely know about myself, others, and this life, that make me unreasonably happy. By the time we are done, you'll know them too, and these truths will sink deep inside you and transform your relationship with this life.

You are phenomenal! You're exciting! You're ridiculously sassy! Your thinking is fresh and vibrant! Your ideas are intense and full of idealism! I'm sure you know everything, but I've met with thousands of people like you, and I know that your heart is soft and willing to hear and accept truth when you hear it. You are truly the hope of this world!

I don't know where you are or where you've been, but all I need to know from you is this: **Do you want to have a great life? Do you want to do and feel great?** Then I'm your man—I can help. If you want to live the good life, a life rich with excitement, love, joy, and meaning, then read and re-read these pearls of wisdom until they become written in your mind and heart. Experiment with them until they become engraved in your personal character.

Think of life as a lab. You're the scientist, running the experiments. **Your mistakes aren't terminal. Your successes**

aren't final. Try different things. Mix it all up. Let's see what you can come up with! With your mind and my brawn, we'll be unstoppable! Come on, take a chance and pick through this book. My sincere desire is that it will become a source of wisdom, encouragement, and hope for you.

Your friend,
Iuri T. Melo

INTRODUCTION
PSYCHOLOGY 101 - UNDERSTANDING YOUR SELFIE

Welcome to class! Don't freak out, this won't be like any class you've ever been to. In a page or two, I will help you realize why you do the things you currently do, how you can make real life changes whenever you desire and, most importantly, how to be happier now and tomorrow. There are three things you will understand by the time I'm done with you:

1. You have a brain (really?)! You also have a mind, and they are not the same thing. I will show you how to use your mind to transform your brain into a fantastic tool.

2. How to change and improve any behavior in a profound and long-lasting way. You and your future spouse can thank me later.

3. How to become full of mind, or mind-full. These days, being mind-full is all the rage! Anyone who is anyone is talking about it: "Be mind-full when you eat," "Be mind-full when you go to the bathroom." People are crazy! I'll show you how to understand and use this skill in a way that will empower you. Ready? Let's hit it!

LET ME DEFINE MIND-FULLNESS FOR YOU

To be mind-full is to be aware, deliberate, and congruent. You must possess and train these 3 skills to become mind-full, instead of mind-less, or what I like to call brain-full.

1. **Become Aware**: Becoming aware simply means that **you see more of what is happening**. You look a little deeper into yourself, circumstances, and others. The goal is to see beyond the surface, and discover the gold that is inherent in every situation and person. **As you become more and**

more aware, you won't judge a book by its cover, simply because you realize that there is so much more. Awareness will train you to be patient, because you must pause your initial judgment of people and things while you seek for additional information so that you can make a more accurate judgment. **Not only will awareness cultivate the divine attribute of patience, but it will ultimately yield the fruit of understanding, and finally, compassion.** To activate awareness, simply ask yourself the question, "What am I missing right now?", then open your eyes to see new things in yourself, others, and the miraculous environment around you.

2. **Be Deliberate:** Being deliberate simply means that you **act and do things on purpose.** Training yourself to do this begins with the realization that we are not deliberate much of the time (you'll learn a bit more about this later). Being deliberate means to act and do things because they are helpful and effective. You're not a broken record or some piece of flesh that simply repeats things. You do things in the moment that are wise and meant to promote your freedom, happiness, fun, friendship, peace, growth, and hope. That, my friend, is how you learn to become deliberate. Look at events in the moment, and not simply as shadows of the past. **Act deliberately and resist the natural urge to be robotic.** Decide here and now that you want to "suck out all the marrow of life" in every moment! You won't be able to do that if you're running around on autopilot. **Do things because they are intelligent. Do them because they will bring you joy both in the present and the future. Act in ways that promote excitement, love, and hope in yourself and others around you.** If you are not doing this, you are already caught up in toxic and unhelpful patterns that will only bring you further misery. STOP! Begin to practice being more deliberate today. Ask yourself: "Will this help me? Will this promote joy, peace, and friendship? Is this smart?" And then make a better choice. Enjoy.

3. **Be Congruent**: Look, here is the straight-up truth. You're not just a mammal or some lower creature with a brain. You are a spiritual being constantly needing to grow and evolve. You cannot escape this internal and divine call. This is what you are meant to do! **You will find that happiness, joy, and fulfillment naturally result when you are being creative and expanding your life and abilities. Being congruent, then, simply means that what you do is in line with your highest self, or the divine you! Being rude, manipulative, bitter, resentful, unforgiving, rigid, entitled, or mocking others will not, and cannot, bring you joy and confidence, because it goes against your highest self. You cannot betray others and be happy, because you are betraying your highest self - period!** You may feel momentarily powerful, proud, or superior, but any intelligent individual can easily see that this is not happiness nor peace. In fact, it is the recipe for a life of insecurity and misery. So seek for the highest, most beautiful characteristics, and slowly work on developing an outstanding character. Start with kindness. Try on humility. Exercise thankfulness. Listen to others and become understanding and compassionate. Forgive your parents and siblings. Start there, and then throw in a little courage to the mix to help you act these out.

The Brain and the Mind

The brain and mind work kind of like your phone. Your mind is what you see. It's the icons, buttons, and apps that you can open and interact with. Your brain is the phone's operating system. It's the stuff that's running underneath the screen that you can't see and probably don't have a clue about. You just press the button, and it's there! It's a little like magic.

Your brain and mind are much the same. You are mostly aware of what you are thinking, feeling, and doing. You can walk this way, talk this way, change directions, look somewhere else. This is the conscious you, the mind-full you. Your brain is the part inside of you that makes all of this work effortlessly. It's the unconscious you, the brain-full you. You don't have to think about walking, talking, writing, whistling, running, jumping, focusing, because your brain has mastered and learned how to do all that stuff. **Your brain is freaking amazing!** If you didn't have one, you would definitely want to buy one on Amazon.

HERE ARE A FEW THINGS YOU MAY WANT TO KNOW ABOUT YOUR BRAIN:

- **Your brain is a survival mechanism:** The main purpose of your brain is to keep the rest of the organism safe (hint: you are the organism). **It does this by moving you away from anything that it perceives is painful or potentially harmful toward something that it believes is safe and comfortable**. In a sense, your brain is driven to protect you, but sometimes it doesn't do a good job. Sometimes, in an effort to protect you, and move you toward comfort, your brain may appear to drive you toward dishonesty, sex, needy behavior, manipulation, pity, lying, anger, destructive friendships, etc. The brain is trying to be helpful by moving you toward something that it believes is comfortable, but in the end it becomes tragic and harmful. In addition, because the brain loves repetition and patterns, it will sometimes keep you away from trying new things, or taking risks, because that's simply not part of the program. You see the issue? Life's purpose is your personal evolution and growth, but sometimes your brain's tendencies (remember, away from danger, and toward comfort) keeps you from asking that girl out, or leaving your mean and abusive friends, or working out a problem simply because it feels scary. Fear, you will discover, is a most interesting and difficult emotion to deal with. **I will show you how to train your brain to do something that is awesome now and super helpful in the long run as well.**

- **Your brain will do what you consistently and repeatedly ask it to do:** You probably didn't realize that

6

you had that kind of relationship with your brain, but in the long haul, **your brain will become a physical representation of your choices.** It's just what it is! Recorded within the grooves of your brain will be all of the choices you have made. Do something for long enough, and it becomes a nice little pattern, with a bow on top. Now don't freak out—**you are made to change and evolve. Change is certain and absolutely natural** (you can't help it). So if you've already got some habits that you're not particularly loving, we can work to change those.

- **Your brain is amoral ("What the...?"):** Your brain doesn't care if things are right or wrong. Your brain's main job is to create patterns. A pattern is turning something complex into a shortcut. Walking, playing an instrument, and writing, are all great examples of this. Take driving, for example: you have to move your hands just right, press the gas pedal with just the right amount of pressure, keep your eyes focused not only on what you are doing but on all of the traffic around you as well, press the clutch, brake, and accelerator at just the right amount. When you first begin to drive, all of this will feel a bit clunky and overwhelming (albeit kind of exciting), but over time, this massively complex pattern will become almost completely unconscious, meaning that your brain will just do it all for you, and you won't even have to bother thinking about it. Instead, you will be laughing with your friends, or singing your lungs out while driving down the road. Know this: **Whatever you repeatedly do, your brain will master and turn into a shortcut and, equally important, your brain will always choose the shortcut, unless persuaded and taught to do otherwise.** Your brain will just as easily create a shortcut for using and abusing marijuana, drinking, smoking, creating drama, or looking at pornography, as it will to exercising, being kind, learning math (yes, I said math, fool!), mastering an instrument, riding a bike, rock climbing, mastering a sport, or just about any activity. See, I told you it was amazing!

- **Your brain is plastic:** Actually, the term that really smart and snooty people use to describe this phenomenon is neuroplasticity. All this means is that the brain is in flux all the time, and throughout your life. **The brain is constantly adapting, expanding, and trimming. Whatever you introduce to your brain is recorded. Whatever you repeatedly expose it to will likely become a pattern. Whatever you neglect gets trimmed or cut out and loses its sway on you.** Imagine a jungle in front of you. You have a large machete (big freakin' knife), and you begin to carve a path through this jungle. You repeat this same route, continuing to cut through vegetation, and trodding through leaves and dirt. After a little while, the route appears as a path (brain pattern) through the jungle. This is like your brain. Sometimes these are really nice and effective patterns (waking up early, exercising, being patient, loyal, and honest). Other times (casual sex, self-loathing, neediness, jealousy, drugs, alcohol, dishonesty) they are not! So, pick up your machete, maybe get some good advice and support from people who care about you, and head to the jungle to carve a new path. You may find yourself wandering back through that old path again, but don't fret or fear, because this isn't a fatal failure, it's a necessary part of the process—simply turn your body around and begin to carve a better path, until it becomes a natural part of you. Over time, you will look at that jungle, and you will notice those old childish, insecure, and immature paths become overgrown and reclaimed by the jungle. **That, my friend, is your brain on change. There is no other word to describe it other than miraculous!**

- **The brain loves to generalize:** This one is a classic idea that is important for you to understand. The brain simply believes that things that happened in the past will likely occur in the future. **The brain's motto is, "If it happened then, it will happen now, and it will happen again." The problem of course is that this is**

not true! Just because you've been hurt before doesn't mean that it will happen again. Just because some boy rejects you once doesn't mean it will happen every time. Just because you have failed at something doesn't mean that you're destined to fail for the rest of your life. See what I'm saying? This becomes even more difficult because whatever you feel in your brain shows up (or manifests) in the body. So your *past* failures or hurts show up as powerful fear emotions in the body *now*. Remember that your brain is not the enemy. You don't have to treat it as an adversary. It's just trying to protect you from feeling pain again. With a little patience and persuasion, you can encourage your brain to attempt risky things that are important and meaningful, and to take a few steps beyond the box you're in.

- **Your brain sees what it believes:** This is a pretty trippy thing the brain does. **Your brain is constantly seeing and seeking what you believe is happening**. For example, if you believe, "My school is full of losers and stuck-up people", guess what your brain will find for you? Yup, you got it, your brain will make sure you notice everything that goes wrong at school. If you believe, "I'm no good, and no one likes me", guess what your brain will see? Indeed, your brain will gather evidence to confirm that that is exactly who you are, and how others see you. If you believe, "My parents are idiots", let's be honest, they might be (lol), but the point is that your brain will constantly work to prove that concept for you. This is one of those brain-full patterns that you must be aware of and mind-fully work to change. You can do this by **realizing that there is always more than what you see. Always!**

HERE ARE A FEW THINGS YOU MAY WANT TO UNDERSTAND ABOUT YOUR MIND:

- **Your mind is driven by love and purpose:** Even though the brain loves to be pleased, comforted, and entertained, the mind will not, and cannot, be satisfied by mere primitive drives and desires. The ultimate and sincere desires of the mind are to learn to love, to expand and evolve toward your highest self (grow UP!), and to be congruent with your highest values. Maslow (old psychologist dude) famously said, **"What a man/woman can be, they must be." That, of course, is true. You will certainly not grow happy while pursuing base-level desires**. You may be comfortable or distracted for a while, but **true joy comes only by pursuing a path in life that is righteous and truly worthwhile.**

- **Your mind requires focus and energy:** Your *brain* runs automatically (remember, it's the unconscious—old patterns and habits), but **your *mind* requires attention and focus**. Take, for example, your brain's need to make quick judgments about people and circumstances. Your brain will do this about everything! It will decide for you what is important and what is not. It will make quick judgments about people and circumstances. Some of these will occasionally be somewhat accurate, but often they will not. This is where your focus, attention, and energy need to come in and slow the brain down a bit. So when my brain says, "Iuri, this means that... That means this... That person is this... That person is that...", I turn on my mind and say, "Now, hold on, let's **(1) suspend the judgment, (2) gather more information, (3) and make a better, more accurate judgment of the situation**." Remember that the brain loves to generalize. You can resist that brain-full pattern by focusing and using your energy to slow the heck down. This will help you make intelligent decisions that are based on current information and overall life experience.

- **Your mind is responsive:** As you learn to turn your mind "ON," you will become more responsive to life (making wise and deliberate choices), instead of reactive (acting and doing things without thought). The *brain* is reactive and will often choose the path of least resistance (remember, it functions on old patterns and habits), but the *mind* has the ability to respond to situations based on what is happening right now, and considering what is truly important for you. **Your power and success in life lies in your ability to awaken this great power. This great power lies somewhere between what happens to you, and what you do. It is the God-given ability of choice!** Now this may seem obvious, but it is supremely powerful. **Your life, you see, will turn on very small hinges. Seemingly small choices combine over time to form huge mountains**. So get your mind "ON" and choose wisely, my friend!

- **Your mind is flexible**: Your *mind* has the ability to see things beyond hot or cold, black or white, happy and sad. Your *brain* is rigid and somewhat impatient. It sees people in very black or white ways. It sees events and classifies them very quickly: "This is good, this is bad." As you expand your ability to be mind-full, you will increase your ability to be flexible and dynamic in life. You'll look beyond good and bad and seek to understand. You'll look deeper than happy and sad and realize that between those two distant points there is a whole universe of emotions that matter as well. Later on in the book (Chapter 1), you'll read one of my favorite little stories, which is sure to become one of yours as well, that will illustrate this idea for you. **One of the great signs of maturity is the ability to adapt and discover the beauty and meaning in circumstances and events.** Rigid individuals are stubborn, inflexible, and moody. They don't adapt well to change. Their rules for what they should be doing, and what others should be doing, are too rigid. As a result they will likely be disappointed, angry, and moody much of the time. **Train your brain to have a little wiggle room. Teach your brain hope. Educate your brain to be humble, soft, and submissive. Train your brain to see individuals beyond good and bad, and instead see them as equals, just trying to make sense**

of this life. Become a little more elastic and you'll find yourself much happier and at peace.

- **Your mind is progressive**: Your brain loves to identify with things. Chances are that your brain has gotten hold of you and thrown some labels at you that have already stuck:

  - "I'm a night person"; "I'm not a morning person"
  - "I'm not good at math (or some other subject)"
  - "I'm not athletic/pretty/smart/outgoing"; "I'm shy/ugly/dumb/a homebody"
  - "I'm depressed/anxious"; "I've got this or that"
  - "I'm not this or that"; "I'm this or that"

That's just what your brain loves to do. It loves to define things quickly. Here's the magnificent truth, though: you are none of those things! **You are a work in progress! You are truly evolving. Don't define yourself and others so quickly.** Give yourself a little time to breathe, and allow yourself the freedom to try lots of things. Just because you've had a bad experience with one thing or another doesn't mean you won't enjoy it or become fantastic at it. So remember this: your brain will try to shrink you down to some definition of who you are, but you no longer need to listen to that, because you now know the truth: **you are evolving all the time and are not meant to be contained**.

Extremely short summary so we can get on with it:

Become more mind-full! Become less mind-less! Less robotic, more deliberate and with eyes open. Less rigid, more flexible—with yourself and others. Slow down your judgments, and take a bit more time with people, and then make a judgment that is good for you. Don't let your brain pigeonhole you into some identity—you are eternal and constantly evolving. Don't let fear drive your life. Instead, let love and the pursuit of truth guide your steps. Focus your attention on becoming less proud and insecure. Admit that you are a fool, and work on being humble and willing to make lots of mistakes. Instead of condemning others, be more forgiving of their errors in judgment. Be gentle, loyal, and patient with yourself (and others).

Some final words. Read them if you like:

I just love you! I know that may sound a little odd (or creepy), but I do. I love being around teens and adolescents. Your craziness speaks to me! Besides the fact that I was one of you a few moons ago, I've had thousands upon thousands of opportunities to listen to you and your personal stories of success, tragedy, joy, and great sadness. I've been a therapist for 14 years now. I've dealt with so many teens in part because of the type therapy that I do. My kind of therapy is rock climbing, bouldering, rappelling, and canyoneering. I have found that teens would rather do therapy with me on the sheer rock cliffs of Southern Utah than talking and philosophizing with me in my office. I don't blame you—I would too! We climb, then talk, then climb some more. The process is a little bit like magic. The outcome is you become physically stronger, psychologically wiser, and a real-deal legit climber.

This book is for you and, in a very real sense, *by* you. The stories, wisdom, and experiences that I'm sharing with you all had their genesis in real-live sessions with teens. I plead with you as a dear friend would, please, *please* read and learn from each one of these tips. **Don't be like the Titanic, bouncing around from iceberg to iceberg, only to yell out, "Life Sucks!"** Well, it most certainly does, and it will continue to suck until you (and I) **learn how to sail like a boss**. That's the deal. I'm not going to tell you that what you do doesn't matter, because my experience—and the experiences of thousands of teens—screams that it does.

I promise I won't talk down to you. I won't treat you like a child. **Teens have changed the course of history, and you can, too! You're not here just to be entertained and babysat. Your ability and passion are what make you so absolutely valuable right now!** Your value is unlimited in your home, school, church, and community. You can walk into a room and change the mood in that room. You can help your parents in ways that you may not realize. Your influence on your brothers and sisters is so critically important. **Your voice matters. Your actions matter (to you and others). Your ideas are valuable**. I'm not trying to burden you with responsibility—I'm just speaking the truth as clearly as I can. **You're either consciously making this world extraordinary or unconsciously going around hurting yourself and others**. I've done my share of hurting myself and others (unfortunately, I'm not done yet), but I'm trying to learn. Hopefully, you can learn as well.

So what do you say? Are you ready to learn the art of happiness? Are you ready to become a humble giant? It doesn't matter where you are or where others are—you and I begin right here. Let's do this!

Awesome Advice About Life

Chapter 1
Good Luck, Bad Luck...I Don't Know

Once there was a farmer. He owned a simple farm with his one son. They owned a single horse. One day the horse ran away. The neighbors immediately came over lamenting, "Oh, what terrible luck. Your one horse ran away! What terrible luck." The farmer calmly responded, "Maybe." Three days later, the horse returned—and brought with it three wild horses. The neighbors exclaimed,; "What great luck— your one horse, plus three more! What great luck!" The farmer simply responded with, "Maybe." A week later, the farmer's son was riding one of the wild horses, attempting to break it in, when the horsebucked him off, breaking his leg. The neighbors returned. "What terrible luck! What great misfortune!" The farmer answered, "Good luck, bad luck....I don't know." A few weeks later, the Chinese army passed by drafting young men to go to the front lines. They saw the young man with the broken leg and said, "Well, he's got a broken leg; we can't take him." So they passed him over. Ecstatic, the neighbors exclaimed,, "What great luck! What great fortune!" To which the farmer simply responded, "Maybe."

This is one of my favorite stories. Remember it, and perhaps work on becoming a bit more like this wonderful farmer. This humble man had a wonderful and mind-full ability to do three things:

- **Suspend his judgment:** He was able to see events happen in his life without casting immediate, drama-filled judgments (unlike the neighbors). Perhaps you know people like the neighbors in this particular story—perhaps you're like them. Observe your brain's urge to immediately classify things, "This means this; that means that," then use your mind to settle your brain, and slow that judgment down.

Remember, life is 1% what happens to you, 99% what you do with it. This skill will allow you to respond mindfully to things, instead of reacting mind-lessly to life. Take your time with things, and allow other people time as well. Perhaps try asking people around you who are wise and care for you what they think something means. Don't force drama; instead be emotionally mature and give yourself and others a break.

- **Accept events as they happen:** Look, there is no doubt that many great things will happen to you, as well as some very undesirable things. I want you to know, in the strongest yet gentlest way that I can say, that **every moment can become a source of power and wisdom.** That is an unbelievably powerful doctrine, and there are people throughout history who have taken the horror that life has thrown at them and have found a way to convert it into preparation, wisdom, forgiveness, and love. I have no doubt that you will be able to do the same. **No life event is wasted on you! With acceptance comes the ability to cultivate understanding, and with understanding comes wisdom.** This farmer was wise.

- **Keep on living:** Because he didn't get wrapped in the things he couldn't control, this farmer quietly went about doing what mattered instead of becoming bitter and irritated by the events of his life. His focus was on responding wisely and deliberately to the events of his life instead of complaining about them. He didn't get caught up asking, "Why me?" Instead he focused on, "What can I do now?" And that is the key.

Look, I have no idea who you are, or what your life has been like. I wish I could be present and help you individually. Perhaps you've had some tragic things happen to you. Perhaps you struggle with depressive or anxious thoughts and feelings. Maybe you're overly insecure and driven by fear. Perhaps you've done some things that make you cringe. We all carry the burden that life inflicts upon us, but with this new understanding comes the ability for us to continue on and try different things. **You no longer have to remain mired and stuck in the quicksand of events. You can get out and continue, because you now know that even the weakest of things can become strong.**

Don't get stuck in questions like "Why me?" because that's an absolutely terrible question! Why not you? A much better approach is to ask, "Now what?," then moving forward and taking small steps that will allow you to move beyond those things that hold you prisoner. Some of you may need to be brave enough to talk to a parent, a therapist, or a religious leader for some assistance. Do it, and remember the old farmer, "Maybe."

LIFE HACK #1
10 SECONDS BEFORE LEAVING A HOT SHOWER,
TURN THE WATER TO COLD FOR AN EXTRA BOOST OF ENERGY!

CHAPTER 2
SAY YES!

Have you ever heard of a man called Henry David Thoreau? Didn't think so. Well, he was a philosopher/ poet/many other things. He lived in the mid 1800's, and at one point he decided that he would leave his home and town and move to a small, rudimentary (no wi-fi, electricity, or hot water) cabin by the shores of Walden Pond. He lived there on-and-off for 2 years, and ultimately wrote a book about his experience called *Walden*. Within this book is my very favorite quote of all time. I first heard it when I watched the movie "Dead Poets Society," and ever since it has remained my favorite quote. Now that I think about it, it has also become a bit of a personal motto. Without further ado, here it is:

*"I went to the woods because I wished to **live deliberately**, to front only the essential facts of life and see if I could not learn what it had to teach, and not, when I came to die, discover that I had not lived. **I did not wish to live what was not life, living is so dear**; nor did I wish to practise resignation, unless it was quite necessary. I wanted to **live deep and suck out all the marrow of life**, to live so sturdily and Spartan-like as to put to rout all that was not life, to cut a broad swath and shave close, to drive life into a corner, and reduce it to its lowest terms."*

What part sticks out to you? Which part did you enjoy the most? For me, it has always been, "I wanted to live deep and suck out all the marrow of life." That's what this chapter is all about. Sucking the marrow! Taking the very best that life has to offer, and doing it deliberately.

If it's good, new, exciting, adventurous, leads you to being healthier, is reasonably safe, potentially fun, and

legal (you didn't think I was going to forget that one), DO IT! SAY YES!

- Want to go work out? "I don't want to be sore...YES!"
- Want to go for a walk? "Sounds boring...YES!"
- Want to go do something fun? "Could be dangerous...YES!" (Keep it reasonably safe.)
- Want to go bowling? "Probably jam my finger on the ball...YES!"
- Want to go on a hike? "I hate the heat...YES!"
- Want to hang out? "I have to catch up on my Instagram...YES!"
- Want to go smoke some weed? "Hmm...NO!" (Just testing you to see if you were awake.)
- Want to wake up at 6 a.m and see the sunrise? "My bed is so comfy...YES!"
- Want to go rock climbing? "I'm terrified of heights...YES!"

You get the point: **Say YES to living deep and experiencing the totality of life.** Give yourself a chance to grow, expand, and be happy. That is the stuff of life! Of course you have responsibilities, chores, school to work on, and other commitments. Say YES to those things as well, and then get your tush off the couch, your eyes away from the TV or your phone, and get busy living! Make it a habit to say YES to trying out new things and expanding your horizons. Now get out there and start saying YES!

LIFE HACK #2
"LIFE IS EITHER A DARING ADVENTURE OR NOTHING."
-HELEN KELLER

CHAPTER 3
THE BEAM IN YOUR EYE

A worried mother came to Gandhi and said, "Gandhi, would you please tell my child to stop eating sugar?" Gandhi responded, "Bring him back in a month." The woman left a bit confused but did as Gandhi suggested and brought her son back a month later. Ghandi took the boy by the hands and said, "Stop eating sugar!" Somewhat annoyed, the mother asked, "Why didn't you tell that to my son a month ago?" to which Gandhi replied, "a month ago, I was still eating sugar."

I'm not sure what you believe about Jesus, but I'm utterly fascinated by His life and the things He taught and said. Among the many of His sayings stands this powerfully simple teaching:

"And why beholdest thou the mote [small speck of wood] that is in thy brother's eye, but considerest not the beam [big fat piece of wood] that is in thine own eye? Or wilt thou say to thy brother, let me pull the mote out of thine eye; and, behold, a beam is in thine own eye? Thou hypocrite, first cast out the beam out of thine own eye; and then shalt thou see clearly to cast out the mote out of thy brother's eye."

The imagery is perfect, and the advice so simple a child could understand it. Here's the deal—our eyes see outwardly, not inwardly, so there is a natural tendency for us to see the weaknesses and faults of others more clearly than we see our own. This mind-less and immature tendency leads us to be critical of others and to blame other people and things for what goes wrong in our lives. These personal blind spots often cause us to judge others incorrectly while completely missing the things we need to work on ourselves.

Here are the three things that Christ and Gandhi are inviting us to learn:

1. Deliberately work at not being a hypocrite.

2. Learn to look and see inside yourself so you can fix your junk. This mind-full skill is called insight, and you'll get better at it as you get older, but start practicing now.

3. As you humble yourself, become aware that you're full of holes, and make an honest effort to work on those areas, you will become better equipped to help others around you.

I'm sure you know people who seem to be especially good at finding fault with others. Perhaps you are this person. It's okay—we can be honest, knowing that as we acknowledge the truth, it gives us power to change. If you find that you are overly critical of your parents, siblings, friends, teachers, or others, it's probably time you take a good look inside, and alter the sensitivity level of your 'fault-finding radar.' **Fault-finding is problematic because it blinds you to your own shortcomings. If this pattern continues, you may experience some self-righteous tendencies and begin to see yourself as better than others. This, of course, is short-sighted, but is a common occurrence that you can correct.** Fault-finding may lead you to begin blaming others for your unhappiness. This will make you grumpy and irritated, because these people around you are making it very hard for you to be happy. It's kind of like saying, "Iuri, your weaknesses are so big that I can't be happy, so "I hate you!" This type of brain-full thinking will bring you significant amounts of bitterness and unhappiness, so let's try something different.

Here are the three things that I suggest you do:

1. When you see others' faults, realize that you've got them, too—they just might have a different name.

2. Be softer and gentler in your critiques of others. This is important because it will teach you to be softer and gentler toward yourself as well.

3. When you see faults in others, find small and simple ways of helping them. Instead of thinking, "Why are you so stupid and weak?," think instead, "Hmm, how can I help?"

As you develop your awareness (ability to see more), and become more skillful at having insight (looking within), you will feel more powerful and able to respond to situations more effectively. This will keep you from feeling hopeless, helpless, and turning yourself into a victim, which is something you definitely don't want to do, as you are about to find out. Ta-ta—for now.

LIFE HACK #3
WANNA HAVE AN AWESOME DAY? MAKE SURE YOU HAVE AN AWESOME MORNING. TRY EXERCISING IN THE MORNING, OR STARTING THE DAY BY READING SOMETHING INSPIRING.

Chapter 4
Refuse to Be a Victim

This chapter is absolutely critical for you, so pull up a chair, turn down the volume, and hear me out. I've been doing therapy now for 14 years, and I constantly watch people make victims out of themselves, and as a result they end up gathering all sorts of misery into their lives. Let me help you to recognize this enormous trap so that you can ultimately avoid it.

First you need to know that there is a difference between being victimized, and making yourself into a victim. The truth is that we are all victimized in many ways in this life. This is reality, and something that must be recognized. Let me give you some examples:

- People will lie to you
- People will cheat you
- People will betray you
- People will take advantage of you
- People will mistreat you
- People will abuse you
- People will treat you unfairly
- You may be born into unfortunate circumstances
- You'll grow up in a small town, or mid-sized town, or big town
- Your parents may divorce

You get the point—there are millions of ways that you can be victimized in this life. Some of you may have even experienced extreme forms of physical, emotional, and/or sexual abuse. Life and people can be terribly tragic. **To you I say: You're amazing. I love you. It won't always be like this (let's make sure it**

isn't). Seek some help, and hang on to some hope, because hope is real.

Life is challenging enough without you having to make it more difficult by making a victim of yourself. Making yourself into a victim means doing these 4 things:

1. **Victims blame other people or circumstances around them.** They are always complaining about something. Here are some simple examples:

   a. My school is stupid.

   b. There's nothing to do—I'm bored.

   c. My teacher is the worst.

   d. My parents don't know anything.

   e. The devil made me do it.

   f. There is nothing to do in this town.

   g. It's raining. It's sunny. It's cloudy. You get the point.

2. **Victims justify their behavior.** When people get caught up in this self-made victim space, I find that they are increasingly defensive, do not take accountability for their mistakes, don't take feedback well, and are always giving excuses for what they've done. Taking ownership or responsibility is not their thing. Here are some examples of this:

   a. I didn't have time to make my bed because I was super busy playing the Xbox.

   b. I would be nice, but my brothers/sisters/parents/friends are idiots.

   c. I would have been home on time, but my watch/phone fell into a sinkhole.

   d. My grades would have been better if my teachers weren't from outer space and complete idiots.

   e. Why should I try hard? No one else is.

3. **Victims act like martyrs.** This is a common trap. They fall into the pity-party mentality. It's the "poor me" attitude. Sometimes people enter this state to get sympathy from others. They commiserate with others to connect with them, and to get a little pat on the back from them. This isn't for you—there are better ways to live your life and to connect with others. Here are some examples of this type of thinking and doing:

   a. My coach doesn't like me.

   b. Nobody talks to me.

   c. I'm just not a smart person.

   d. Nothing ever goes right for me.

   e. Life's just too hard.

4. **Victims make armies.** The old adage "Misery loves company" seems to have some validity to it. Victims love to have other people join forces with them. Whether it's to complain about school, or someone at school, or about how dumb people are, or how unfair life is, or how terrible the lunch at school is, we are constantly seeking for people to enter into our pity party and agree with us. Stop this! Here are some examples:

   a. Oh my gosh! Isn't P.E. just the biggest waste of time? Can you believe I have to change clothes?

   b. The cops in this town are so stupid! Don't you think?

   c. Are you parents as bad as mine?

   d. Can you believe Mr. Peterson gave us homework over the weekend?

   e. Jonny is just so rude and lame, isn't he?

Notice these tendencies in others, and certainly pay attention to see them happening within you. I guarantee you will find them. Some of you might even be quite good at organizing pity parties! No worries—by seeing these things, you can begin to upgrade your "I'm a victim" behavior, and instead become powerful. You see, **the**

biggest problem with being a victim is that the solution to a problem always rests somewhere outside of you. "If only this was that way," or "If I didn't live in such a lame place," or "If only this person wasn't this or that way." Don't you see? **If you are so busy blaming the things outside of yourself, you are neglecting the most important source of power you have— YOU and your ability to change and influence any situation.**

The title of this chapter is "Refuse to be a victim" because the reality is that you and I are going to slip into this dark and useless pit at times. Honestly, there are times when you will be drawn to this type of behavior. It's crazy but it's true. My hope is that as you begin to notice it in yourself and others, you will be able to do it less, and thus increase your ability to take valuable and powerful action, instead of feeling and believing that you are the pinball in a sick pinball game. Now go, and git 'er done!

LIFE HACK #4
SOMETIMES YOU SMILE BECAUSE YOU'RE HAPPY.
SOMETIMES YOU'RE HAPPY BECAUSE YOU SMILE.
GO ON! SMILE AND BE HAPPIER!

CHAPTER 5
PRACTICE EXCELLENCE, NOT PERFECTION

Hey good lookin', what you got cookin'? Lovely to see you again. Perfectionism can be one of those personal habits that just make a mess of your psychology and emotions. Let me explain. The messages of perfectionism go something like this:

- I can only feel good about something if it's perfect (ridiculous).

- I can only turn in this homework if it's done perfectly (recipe for disaster).

- If I can't do it perfectly, then I'm not doing it at all (bull-honkey!).

- Unless I look, weigh, or perform in a perfect way, I won't be happy (you got that right— you won't be happy with this kind of thinking).

Some people are more likely to think this way. Sometimes we develop this disastrous kind of thinking all by ourselves, other times we have parents who are so focused on perfection and performance that we end up believing that that's how life is, and how we ought to think about ourselves. The major problem with perfectionism is that it's unattainable, at least in this life. See the problem? **If what you are trying to reach is constantly impossible, the only possible outcome is disappointment.** Now, I'm not suggesting you aim low, or become satisfied by a life of mediocrity—heavens no! **What I am suggesting is for you to engage in whatever it is that you are doing, practice it, learn it, dive deep into it, learn the ins and outs of it, and reap the amazing benefits of mastery and excellence.**

Do you play an instrument? Quit being a dead weight and complete pain in the rear to your parents, and get busy practicing becoming excellent at it (your older self, future family and children will thank you for it). I promise you that this skill will come in very handy in your life and provide you with hours of enjoyment, if only you will take the time to develop some mastery, and get into the guts of it.

Play a sport? Don't waste your time and that of your coach dilly-dallying and picking daisies at practice. Work hard! **Develop an inspiring work ethic and an awesome attitude while doing increasingly hard things.** As you do this you will feel more motivated and inspire others around you to perform at a higher level. **I guarantee that it's possible for you to have an amazing and fun time while practicing like a boss!** Mediocre effort won't bring you joy or make you look cool—it will instead turn you into a little resentful pain-in-the-butt that doesn't understand why they don't like what you're doing.

Going to school? Now, school matters for a lot of different reasons, and the most important of those is for you to **train your brain to love learning** (remember, your brain will learn whatever you consistently ask it to learn). Seek to learn! Ask for help when you don't understand. Talk to your parents or teachers if you are falling behind (you absolutely must do this, or you'll end up hating school, and everything in it). I've noticed that as people begin to fail or struggle in school, they turn themselves into bona fide self-made victims ("School is stupid"; "Teachers are dumb"; "School is not for me"; "I'm not smart enough"; "I'm not going to be using this stuff anyway."—don't be ridiculous!). I know this happens, because it happened to me (I guess it takes one to know one). Get a freaking tutor/friend/parent to help you! Don't be some insecure little man or woman who doesn't get help because they don't want to look bad—what the...? Come on, your psychology and intelligence is far better than that!

Are you alive and breathing? Get busy sucking the marrow out of life and learning the most critical of all skills—the skill of joy and happiness. **Joy is the ultimate discipline in this life.** How do you do that? Chapter 18 will provide you with some great tools, one of those being the fact that you must invest and engage in your life and in doing the things that are of most value. **You can't trick joy!**

Shortcuts will yield short and small outcomes for you. Reap success by sowing success. If you want something, go and get it, period! Don't sit around in the harbor waiting for your ship to come in, to have it roll out the red carpet, and ask you to come aboard. Get in the water and go get it!

People who practice excellence understand that **life functions line upon line, precept upon precept, here a little, there a little, small by small, slow by slow.** This is the pattern. Because they comprehend this simple truth, they develop patience and perseverance. **Your brain and body can be taught to do the most remarkable things. We are absolutely miraculous! Don't let your perfectionistic thoughts and ideas paralyze you or drive you to become a total nincompoop to yourself and others. Excellence is trying, learning, evolving, and ultimately improving.** If you are only satisfied when you arrive at perfection, then get ready to be miserable! Pursue excellence instead and reap the fruits by and by! Start where you are today, not where you wish you could be. Well done, another chapter bites the dust. Go on, read the next one!

Life Hack #5
"Fall seven times, stand up eight."
- Japanese Proverb

CHAPTER 6
NEVER SAY THE F-WORD OR THE D-WORD

Now, before you begin to think that I'm just a total wacko (too late, hmm?), the F-word is the word "Fair." The D-word is "Deserve." Go ahead and just completely erase these useless, inaccurate, and poisonous words from your vocabulary.

My poor kids (I have 5 of them) can't even say, "Dad, that's not fair," or "You're not being fair," because my answer to them is, "I don't do fair!", or "I don't even believe in fairness or that word altogether, so I just don't know what the heck you're talking about." **Fairness is a false construct, a false idea that twists your perception of reality.** Fairness just straight-up doesn't exist! Maybe you can think of some idealistic scenario where fairness occurs—I just don't know where that is. The reason I'm telling you this is because you absolutely must **shift your focus away from fairness, and instead just do the best you can at doing the right thing!** Sometimes the right thing will look like "fairness," but many times it will not. That's perfectly fine, because you no longer have to believe in the concept of fair. Never, ever, no, never use it again!

Think about it for a sec, what's "fair"? Is it the fact that you were born into a well-to-do family? The fact that you were born in America, Europe, Africa? Into poverty or wealth? That you can think clearly or that you have a mental handicap? That you can see or that you are blind? **Fairness just doesn't compute, and it's not intelligent, so stop sounding unintelligent by using that word to complain, manipulate, or explain something that is happening.** For those of you who are Christian, think of Christ and the suffering that He underwent for each one of us. His sacrifice is the most unfair act in history! He, sinless, paid for the sins of every sinner!

If the concept of "fair" is unhealthy and unintelligent, the idea that we "deserve" something is even more twisted. "I deserve to be happy!" "I deserve to get an A," "I deserve to be treated with respect," "I deserve to be in the starting lineup, instead of sitting on the bench," "I deserve to be liked," "They deserved every bit of what they got." Just give it up already! Once again we are dealing with an incorrect construct—that somehow these things are owed to us! **No one owes you anything; the reality is that we are all massively indebted!** What can you say instead of "I deserve?" Say instead, "I'm worthy of happiness, and I'll do the best I can to live the kind of life that will create it." Say instead, "I'm worthy of respect, and when I act in a respectful manner, I invite the respect of others, thus making it more likely that I will be respected." "I'm worthy of love, and as I become loving to others, I increase the likelihood that others will be loving back to me." Being worthy in the way that I'm using the word is something that we're born with. **We are all worthy to receive both sunshine and rain in this life. Instead of a mindset focused on deserving, nurture the psychology of gratitude. Discover what each moment has for you, how it can prepare you and help you evolve.**

Words matter! It's the only way we have to describe the reality we inhabit. When you get stuck in a mindset of "It's not fair," or "I deserve," you will be unhappy. Let's cultivate an internal environment where joy and peace can exist. The erroneous concept of fairness and the "I deserve" mentality corrupt us, so join me in striking these words from your internal dictionary. Good luck and have fun explaining this to your children.

LIFE HACK #6
"LOVE THE LIFE YOU LIVE. LEAD THE LIFE YOU LOVE."
-BOB MARLEY

CHAPTER 7

"WHATEVER," "I DON'T KNOW," "I DON'T CARE," AND OTHER LIES YOU TELL YOURSELF

Hey there! Wow, you look amazing! I hope life is treating you well! Let's talk words for a moment. I understand that the words in the title are just figures of speech (things we say), but perhaps we can learn to communicate and express ourselves a little more accurately, because the reality is that we absolutely care. **Words matter, and what you say absolutely matters!** I work with married people every day who come to me for counseling because they are fighting, or not getting along well. Guess what people always say they want to improve? Yup, their communication. "We just don't communicate well." "He doesn't listen." "She's too critical." "He doesn't care." And on and on! I'm telling you these things so that you can avoid some of the potholes of life.

"WHATEVER"

"Whatever" is the verbal equivalent of rolling your eyes. In fact, you may not even be able to say the word without rolling your eyes. The messages that are being communicated when we say *whatever* are these:

- You're an idiot, but go on and do what you're going to do!
- Whatever it is that you do, I don't care.
- I don't agree with you or what you are about to do.
- Your ideas are stooopid!

Now, "whatever" can be a harmless word. It can even be used in an endearing and fun way. I'm telling you this because I quite enjoy using that word. I'm warning you because I have used that word insultingly as well. Chances are you've used it both ways, too. If you are playing around with your buddies, use "whatever" freely. If you are having a serious conversation with adults, or parents, or your friends; if important ideas or opinions are being shared, "whatever" is not a good idea. **Be the kind of individual who gives respect to others. It will earn you many friends, and keep many, too. Listen to people's ideas and opinions. Respectfully disagree, but don't just push it aside and stomp on it by saying "whatever."** Say this instead:

- You know, I don't think the same way.

- I respectfully disagree. What do you think about…?

- It's your call. I'm not sure it's a great idea.

- Can you tell me again why you're doing what you're doing?

"I DON'T KNOW"

"I don't know" is one of my very favorites. Teenagers and adolescents are the kings and queens of "I don't know." Most of the times when you say "I don't know," what you really mean is:

- "I don't want to think about it."

- "I don't care about what you're asking me."

- "I can't be bothered by your meaningless questions."

- "I'm lying" ("I don't know" is a great way to hide the truth— yeah, right!)

I sit across from teenagers all the time and ask them lots of questions. Therapy is a bit threatening, and not the funnest way people can think of to spend an hour of their time (unless they're doing rock-climbing therapy with me!), so when I begin asking them questions about this and that and the other, guess what you guys tell me? Yessiree, "I don't know!" Now, because you are the kings and queens of "I don't know," I've adjusted my questions to sound something like this: "Now, I'm about to ask you a question. Don't answer right away, but think about it for a moment. Sit with the question, and then give me the answer." Or, "Before you say 'I don't know,' just think about what I asked you for a bit, and then tell me what you think."

Saying "I don't know" has likely become a knee-jerk response for you. "You hungry?" "I don't know." "Wanna go do this?" "I don't know." "Do you know?" "I don't know." I love it! So from now on, just **sit with questions for a bit, put on your thinking cap, stretch your mind a bit, and start answering some questions.** It's important because it makes people around you feel valued when you take the time to answer their questions. If you need a little bit of time just say:

- "Hmm... give me a sec."
- "Let me think about that for a minute."
- "Great question!"
- "I don't know, but let me search for it and find out."

"I DON'T CARE"

"I don't care" is the next phrase I hear you use as well. Now, as with all other words, I think this one can be used in the right circumstances as well, although if the conversation has turned a bit for the serious, or if you're talking to a parent, adult, teacher, or religious leader, "I don't care" is not wise. "I don't care" is code for:

- "I'm done talking about this."
- "I don't want to think about this."
- "I'm giving up, you're stupid, and I hate you!"

"I don't care" is usually loaded with resentment and usually means the very opposite of what you are saying. Chances are that you do care, but perhaps you feel like what you say doesn't matter, or that the person hearing you is not really listening or considering what you are saying, which is why you throw up the white flag of "I don't know" and try to get out as quickly as you can. **What you think and say matters, so exercise your assertiveness muscles, and give your opinion.** Try saying this instead:

- "Look, I don't think you understand where I'm coming from. I mean this."

- "I have a thought...how about this?"

- "It's not all about me, but I would prefer this instead."

- "I'm a little bit frustrated. I don't think you are hearing me. Maybe I'm not understanding you very well, either."

Communication just matters. Your words are always loaded with significance, so use them wisely. Remember that many of your relationships hang on how effectively you can communicate. Start practicing today by noticing how often you use these words inappropriately. Use them for fun as well, but when things turn a bit more important, put these words in the closet and bring out your better skills instead. Good luck!

Life Hack #7
"If you're going through hell, keep going."
-Winston Churchill

CHAPTER 8
"I'M HAPPY 'TIL I'M NOT"

Wow, here you are! Smarter, bolder, and better than ever! I just love this phrase, because I find that people today are a bit obsessed with the concept of happiness. Don't get me wrong—I want to be happy, excited, motivated, and confident, but I completely accept that I will not always feel that way, and in addition, the other emotions that I will feel in life matter as well. **You will find that when you greet difficult emotions gently, and with a measure of acceptance, they will pass through you more quickly, and then you will find yourself more peaceful and happy.** The power of "I'm happy 'til I'm not" comes from the knowledge that you don't have to be happy all the time. I think you will find that this is a very freeing concept that will bring you feelings of peace, instead of internal conflict and disappointment.

Now, you may be familiar with the term "emotional intelligence." People are always coming up with smart ideas and phrases to help us understand concepts better. Emotional intelligence has to do with your ability to increase your emotional maturity and endurance. Let me present it to you this way: Imagine a beautiful grand piano, all 88 keys of it. Imagine that each key represents an emotion. All the way from ecstatic, happy, joyous, and curious to frustrated, angry, sad, sorrowful, depressed, fearful, etc. Sometimes people only want to feel the positive emotions in life. In other words, they only want to play the piano's high notes. But what about those wonderful rich tones in the lower end of the piano? And what about playing them together? That is what this quote is all about, and what the concept of emotional maturity is attempting to teach you. **The emotionally mature individual has the increased ability to experience the full spectrum of emotions while staying mind-full (conscious, deliberate, congruent). In addition, the emotionally mature individual recognizes that all emotions**

serve a purpose, even if that purpose is to tell us that
something isn't going quite right. The key here is that you
learn to make peace with your emotions, and to not make
them into your enemy.

Hard-core emotions (anger, fear, jealousy, sadness) are
particularly difficult to deal with, because they have a tendency to
hijack our brains and take over. They overwhelm us, and at times
impact us in such a way that we appear to lose control and act in
ways that are more primitive than intelligent. **Increasing your
emotional intelligence is about taking back some of those
moments and increasing your ability to stay present, and
full of mind during those moments.** I promise it's possible to
do this. In fact, there is a very good chance that this will happen
naturally throughout your life as you mature and become more
insightful. But you can begin now by simply learning to look at
emotions differently and, more importantly, knowing how to
interact with your emotions. **Yes, we can interact with the way
we feel.** I'm the first one to recognize that I don't fully control my
emotions, yet I'm absolutely certain that I can impact them. "How do
I do that?" you ask. There are five ways:

1. **People:** The people who surround us have a tremendous
   impact on what we do and how we feel. When you are feeling
   off, don't isolate and withdraw from others. In fact, do the
   opposite—draw close to those who will support you,
   encourage you to be your highest self, and bring joy and
   humor to your life. It's important to note that we often seek
   people that agree with us, or who are doing the same things
   that we are doing. This is natural, yet it may lead to making
   the same mistakes and getting the same results. It takes
   courage to make a change in friends. If your friends are
   encouraging drug use, illegal behavior, sexual
   experimentation, drama, gossip, or negativity, it's time to
   make a cultural shift and move to a different pond. Be brave
   here. This can be scary and leave you feeling lonely, but it's
   worth it! Be patient, and slowly begin your migration toward
   people who will raise your standard. Better yet, become this
   person yourself.

2. **Psychology:** Your thoughts and the things you are putting into your brain have a gigantic effect on how you feel. For happiness to be a naturally occurring state, you must possess a psychology (beliefs and ideas) that nurtures joy. This psychology must be hopeful, forgiving of self and others, optimistic and proactive ("Good things will come, and I can make them come."), and believing that all things can contribute to my good and experience.

3. **Places:** Sometimes places, smells, and sounds can have a significant impact on how we feel and deal with things. Perhaps you have a favorite spot that speaks peace to your soul, brings calm to your mind, and hope to your heart. Visit that place frequently.

4. **Behavior:** What you do matters and can be a powerful tool in helping you shift through difficult times and emotions when they appear. Running, walking, praying, meditating, exercising, serving and helping others, playing an instrument, listening to music, joining a group of people, catching some sun, even having a shower can dramatically impact your emotional well-being. **Stop fighting the emotions in your head! Use your body to change your brain and the way you feel!** There is no doubt that this works. It may take time, but trust the process. Caution: During difficult times you may feel the urge to "veg out" and distract yourself with a Netflix marathon or the infinite wheel of Instagram. Unfortunately, this will not yield a positive outcome for you. I'm not suggesting we can't ever engage in passive relaxation or entertainment—I'm just encouraging higher level activities for a superior outcome. Your call.

5. **Spirituality:** This term has become a bit watered down and discombobulated as of late. Let me clarify: Spirituality is the recognition and effort we place to connect to the divine that is within us, outside of us, in others, and to the God who created it. It is often connected to religion, because religion is the study and practice of spirituality. Prayer, meditation, and the study of scriptural writings (or other inspired works), has

a supernatural power to impact the totality of our lives. It is my personal advice to you to seek after these things so that you may find them and profit from them.

So if you're not feeling happy all of the time, realize from this moment on that you don't need to be ashamed. This is a very common cycle that people who experience feelings of depression often go through. It looks a little bit like this: they feel sad, then they feel ashamed for feeling sad, which, of course, leaves them feeling even worse. This is the cycle we are attempting to stop. **You can stop this cycle by learning to experience your emotions in a gentle and scientific way.** Think of yourself like a scientist. Notice how your emotions feel in the body. How your thoughts fuel them. Become aware of how your perceptions change and how you react to feelings of sadness, anxiety, and stress. Notice what works and what doesn't. If you are feeling anxious, overly stressed, or depressed for long periods of time, these emotions are a signal to you that something probably needs to get looked at, and that you may need to take action. You might have things going on in life that are creating problems for you. Your thinking may need to get cleaned up a little. It's also possible that you may need to see a therapist or doctor. Be reasonable and mind-full about this. **It is a sign of intelligence to ask for assistance when you need it.** Drop your ego and tell someone who can get you help.

Remember that emotions are signals. They are often manifestations of our personal beliefs about ourselves, others, and the world. When you begin to feel things, train yourself to ask these questions: "What would I have to believe to feel this way?" If you can manage to answer this question, you will now have powerful insight into what is driving your feelings. You can then ask this follow-up question: "What must I realize to feel better?" This is where you train your brain to shift gears and think about solutions, instead of wallowing in the mud. The final question is: "What must I do right now to boost my mood?" When the answers to these questions start coming in, take action! Pay attention, my friend, and do your work!

So, go and be happy! 'Til you're not.'

Life Hack #8

When you meet someone for the first time, repeat their name
inside your head 3 times to help you remember it.

CHAPTER 9
LIVE THE GOLDEN RULE, NOT THE BRONZE RULE

There you are, I hope you are treating life well! So, you may be familiar with the "Golden Rule." The Golden Rule is a terrific tool! It's not easy, but in all honesty, many of the things in life that carry the most value are often not very easy. **The Golden Rule states that we should do unto others as we would have them do unto us. In simpler terms, treat others how you want to be treated.** Now this sounds fine and dandy, but the reality is that we usually don't live the Golden Rule—we instead favor the Bronze Rule! What is the Bronze Rule? The Bronze Rule states that we treat others as they treat us. This may seem like a small difference, but it is completely different. One response is mind-full, the other brain-full. Let me explain the brain-full one first. We have a tendency as humans to be very reactive; we usually reflect what is in front of us. This is very true! A smile promotes a smile; a kind gesture invites a kind gesture in return; forgiveness inspires forgiveness; humor is contagious; anger provokes anger; rudeness provokes rudeness and resentment; defensiveness promotes more defensiveness. I think you get the idea. The brain does a terrific job at reflecting and reacting to what is in front of us.

The time has come for you to graduate from the brain-full response—simply reacting and reflecting—to the higher mind-full living, where you respond to what is being offered based on your highest ideals. The Golden Rule is difficult because it takes effort and presence. It requires you to be awake and conscious so that your responses can be deliberate and based on the wisest ideas in the world! In addition, you must decide what your highest principles are, and believe them independently of others. This means that you do them simply because **you** believe they are the best. Here are some of my own ideals:

- I believe in kindness, because I believe that kind people finish first, and that kindness is better in the short and long run.
- I believe in being loving and friendly.
- I believe in giving people a break, complimenting them, and speaking positively about them.
- I believe in having fun.
- I believe in forgiving myself and others.
- I believe in being patient and compassionate with people.
- I believe that hope is real.

Why don't you take a few moments and decide what your top ten highest ideals are right now, so that you can check yourself, before you wreck yourself!

1.	2.
3.	4.
5.	6.
7.	8.
9.	10.

Remember that learning to respond instead of reacting to situations is a work in progress that is better accomplished by being patient and compassionate (two of my personal beliefs) with yourself and others. I promise that this will not only bring you peace of mind, but a tremendous strength that will be admired by others. I wish you the very best.

LIFE HACK #9
WHEN YOU SHAKE SOMEONE'S HAND, DON'T GIVE THEM A LIMP, DEAD-FISH HANDSHAKE—MAKE IT FIRM AND CONFIDENT.

Chapter 10
3 Questions you Must Master

Howdy partner! I'm about to give you a pearl of wisdom that will build on the last chapter (where we learned about the difference between the Golden Rule and the Bronze Rule), and which will alter the way you perceive your power and influence. You ready? Here it is: **We are constantly inviting and promoting things in our environment and others!** We cannot escape this reality. Here is what this looks like in real life:

- When you smile at someone, you are inviting them to smile back.

- When you are kind, you are literally saying to them, "Let's be kind."

- When you forgive, you are saying, "Let's be forgiving."

- When you are grateful, you are promoting gratitude in others around you.

- When you are friendly, you are saying, "Let's be friendly."

- When you are honest, you are inviting and promoting honesty.

- When you are rude, you are saying, "Let's be rude."

- When you are dishonest, your are inviting dishonesty.

- When you are smug and cold, you are saying, "Let's be smug and cold to each other."

- When you are gossiping and condemning of others, you are saying, "Join me in saying rude things about others and condemning them."

It's a bit scary, isn't it? **You can literally walk into a room and change the feeling in that room. You decide.** You can enter a room and create tension, fear, anger, and coldness, or promote and invite ease, friendliness, safety, love, acceptance, consideration, and happiness. Here is the crazy part: we are always doing this! Whether we think that we are, or that we aren't, it doesn't matter. **We are constantly shaping our environment! We were born to create and, by gum, we will create.**

The three questions that follow are meant to help raise your awareness of what you are inviting and promoting and, most importantly, to improve what you are inviting. Here they are:

1. **"What am I inviting?"** Notice that the question isn't, "What are other people inviting?" It is, "What are *you* inviting and promoting right now?" This question is purposefully designed to turn us inward, because our natural tendency is to notice what others are inviting instead.

2. **"What do I want to invite?"** This question is there to help you remember and reconnect you to your highest values,morals, and goals.

3. **"How do I invite it?"** Well, get busy doing it, that's how! It takes a certain amount of courage and strength to invite those things that are the wisest in the face of disapproval or fear, but I believe that you can and will. Want love? Be loving. Want respect from others? Give it. Want friendship? Be a friend. You get it—if you want something, give that something.

Commit these questions to memory and utilize them often so that they can become a part of your unconscious, thereby becoming automatic. The world is so full of fear, bitterness, selfishness, and anger. Decide today that you will not invite and promote those things with your family, friends, at school, or work, or church, or any other place you find yourself. Your voice matters! Your actions are important! Your effort counts! And yes, you get credit for trying. It's as easy as 1-2-3!

Life Hack #10

When possible, take the scenic route,
and always take the stairs.

Chapter 11
Learn to Work a Problem

Hey, guess what? You are going to experience some extraordinary things in life! You are also going to experience a great deal of tragedy and heartache! Like I said in the Introduction, this life is the full package, and because it is, you must become a master at learning how to work a problem.

I'm reminded of one of my favorite movies, "Apollo 13." This movie tells the true story of the astronauts, and other individuals who were involved in a mission to land on the moon. The mission had such serious problems that they had to forgo the landing on the moon, and it became highly unlikely that the astronauts were going to survive and return home. I'm reminded of when some of the scientist and engineers had gathered together to discuss how to help the astronauts arrive home safely. As the meeting began, a heated argument sprang up and the men lost their focus and vision. They were abruptly brought to task by the project leader, who authoritatively said, "People, let's work the problem!" Even though the astronauts did not land on the moon during that mission, they did return to earth, and the mission was viewed as a success due to the tremendous odds they overcame.

Learn to work a problem! You'll find that many people struggle with the ability to mind-fully focus and work a problem. When problems and difficulties arise, we often behave like the scientists in that movie:

- We yell at each other.

- We make excuses (I bet you're good at this).

- We blame other people.

- We avoid the problem altogether and pretend like it's not happening.

- We pretend like we don't care ("Whatever, I don't care, this is stupid").

- We blame the circumstances around us.

- We blame ourselves (pity party, e.g., "I'm worthless," "I'm a failure," "I'm not very smart").

- We become discouraged and give up.

Einstein humbly stated "It's not that I'm smarter than other people, it's that I stay with a problem longer." Do you hear what he is saying? His ability to stay and linger with a problem longer than other people is what allowed him to ultimately discover the theory of relativity. When I take people bouldering (free climbing) I teach them how to climb, and introduce them to their first "problem." In climbing, a problem is a specific route you are attempting to climb. I've taught thousands of people to do this, and at some point individuals become stuck, or feel like they cannot finish or "solve" the problem. People find all sorts of reasons for why they can't work the problem: "I'm too weak," "I'm tired," "I'm afraid of heights," "The rock is too hot or too cold," "I've never done this before, my hands hurt," or "I don't want to look bad." Whatever the reason, I take people climbing to help them **learn how to stay and work a problem like a BOSS!** My four simple steps are:

1. **See it:** Know where you are and where you are headed.

2. **Think it:** Create a mental strategy and some steps that you can take.

3. **Climb it:** When your hands and feet are on the rock, it's time to climb, not sit and pick daisies.

4. **Fail with style (because you will):** When you fall and fail, do so with style, and rework the problem.

Einstein also stated, "The problems we face cannot be solved at the same level of thinking we were at when we created them." The only way to resolve our present problems is to upgrade our personal psychology. You can do that by using the steps I gave you, free of charge. In fact, your evolution—and much of your happiness—depends upon you working through your personal struggles and difficulties well. So, when you are struggling with your parents, work that problem. When you are failing Math, don't blame the teacher (you know you will), ask for help and work the problem. When your friends desert you, work the problem, and begin investing your time and effort in placing yourself in the right places, with the right people, to make new friendships. Don't get tripped up on what other people think, who did what, whose fault it is, or how life is going to completely fall apart because of your troubles...WORK THE PROBLEM! In a very real way your experiences with school, family, sports, friends, and relationships will either get better or worse based on your ability to work the problem. Well, what are you waiting for? WORK IT!

LIFE HACK #11
"MY LIFE IS MY MESSAGE."
-MAHATMA GHANDHI

Chapter 12
Drugs, Alcohol, and Pornography

I know, I know, you've heard enough about this. Well, maybe you have, maybe you haven't, but stick around for a moment and just hear me out—I promise to be brief. Can I offer you three quick suggestions?

1. If you haven't tried it...don't!

2. If you have tried it...don't try it again!

3. If you're using it often and are finding it difficult to stop...talk to someone, get help, and let's work the problem, right?

The question you may be asking is, "Why?" Lots of people drink, use drugs, smoke cigarettes, use weed, vape, and view pornography. Whether you use those things in your life or not is completely up to you. You are correct—many people experiment with these things, and many others use them regularly. I understand that in the end you get to choose, but I sincerely hope that you don't. I'm not going to give you some sob story about the dangers of those things, because, truthfully, anyone with any sense of themselves, and of the history of humankind, knows that these things are a poison to body, numbing to the heart and, most importantly, they corrupt the brain.

"Yeah, Iuri, but I read this article about this and that, and this one person...blah, blah, blah!" Come on now, if I wanted to go find a research article about how jumping into a field of poison ivy is good for your skin, I could...seriously! Let me give you the two very best reasons why you should consider what I'm telling you:

1. **Because you have a brain.** Let me explain a bit: Your brain, as you have learned from our initial session (Introduction), is a fragile, constantly adapting and evolving creature. It learns everything, remembers everything, and creates shortcuts for everything that relieves pain and moves

us toward relief and pleasure. The problem with drugs is that they do exactly that (and many other things). **Your brain literally becomes the sum of your choices. Your brain will learn whatever you consistently ask it do.** Once the brain creates a shortcut, it always wants to choose the shortcut, no matter how much we mind-fully want to choose something else. Drugs, alcohol, and pornography are chemically engineered to ensnare and trap you. They are not made to be a gentle companion in your life—they are parasites and tigers in a cage that will tear at you wherever and whenever they get a chance. These things are not meant to be domesticated, or managed, because their sole purpose is to alter the mind to the point that you are no longer conscious. **Unconsciousness is the antithesis of your life purpose.** Remember it's not about whether you are strong, or weak, or mature, or young, or old, it's straight up biology and science my friend. **We don't use drugs, alcohol, or view pornography because we realize that we have a brain, and we comprehend what it does.**

2. **Because it is intelligent.** Gaining intelligence and utilizing it in your life is wisdom. Seeking and hungering for intelligence is a magnificent part of our purpose... your purpose. **Consider that "The glory of God is intelligence," thus, your ability to gather information from the most reliable sources, processing it, and making wise judgments is central to your decisions, and more importantly the joy, hope, peace, and happiness that you experience in life**. I gotta be real with you. **You can't do stupid and not feel and think stupid!** Such is life my friend, and as nature teaches us as well, we are constantly sowing and then reaping what we sow.

Anyway, I told you that I would be short, and would not linger and sound like I'm preaching to you. In the end you make the call, you get to choose and pursue the quality of life you want. As your friend I would only say, 'remember that thing that is floating up in your cranium (brain), and be intelligent, the rest is up to you.' **Remember that our goal is to feel life deeply, not numb it out! It is to be become more and more conscious and mind-full, not unconscious and mind-less. It is to be intelligent and wise, not unintelligent and unwise.** Ours is the call to raise humanity, our friends, families, and children to a higher level... this is your birthright, it's what you are called to do. My hope is that you will join me and heed the call. What do you say? It's not even about "just say NO!" it's that these things don't have any significant value that's worthy of consideration. May you choose wisely. Your friend and most strident cheerleader, Iuri Tiago Melo.

LIFE HACK #12
"DO THE DIFFICULT THINGS WHILE THEY ARE EASY AND DO THE GREAT THINGS WHILE THEY ARE SMALL.
A JOURNEY OF A THOUSAND MILES MUST BEGIN WITH A SINGLE STEP."
-LAO TZU

Chapter 13
Feel Good, Do Good
vs.
Do Good, Feel Good

What I'm about to tell you may shock you. I don't want my kids to be happy! I don't want you to be happy, either! "He's certainly lost his mind...Iuri has gone bonkers!" Well, no doubt about that, but let me see if I can make sense of this craziness. I frequently hear people say, "I just want you to be happy," "Just do what makes you happy," "If it feels good, do it," "Feel good first, then do good." Here's the problem with this philosophy: it doesn't work. The pursuit of happiness as the ultimate objective guarantees misery and a very self-absorbed, obsessive search for feelings of happiness in all things. **People act like happiness is the purpose, and it's not. Happiness is an outcome, not a pursuit. Feelings of joy are a product of something else.** When pursued, happiness becomes elusive. Our constant desire to be entertained actually promotes our misery. Have I confused you enough? I hope so, because, my friend, it is the truth. Even though we "are that [we] might have joy" (*Book of Mormon* reference), **happiness and joy are really about the quality of our living, our psychology (the way we interpret life), our daily decisions, and our acceptance of truth.**

So, what do I want my children to do and be? I want them to pursue wisdom. I want them to be honorable. I hope that they will have outrageous fun. I hope that they will seek and find awesome friendships. I hope that they seek and learn goodness, love, truth, and forgiveness, because then, and only then, will they experience a profound joy and a deep meaningful experience here on earth. Only then will their joy be long-lasting, instead of being washed out with every wave or storm that life throws at them. I think you would agree that dishonorable actions, rudeness, isolation, resentment, fear, and selfishness would conversely create the opposite outcome: a life of anger, regret, blame, and loneliness.

So, no—don't just do what makes you happy; instead, do what you believe is the most honorable, loving, intelligent, and progressive thing, and trust the process. I guarantee that, as you refocus your efforts away from your fascination and obsession with being happy all the time, and toward the pursuit of righteous and awesome living, you will mysteriously and curiously find joy flowing out of you effortlessly. It's a strange world we live in isn't it? Do Good=Feel Good, **not** Feel Good=Do Good.

Peace, out...

LIFE HACK #13
NEVER JUDGE A BOOK BY ITS MOVIE, AND ALWAYS READ THE BOOK FIRST.

CHAPTER 14
C.A.S.H. IT!

Show me the money! Okay, I will. Here is a simple tool that you can remember and utilize right away to better the relationships in your life. **My friend, so much of your happiness in this life hinges on the quality of your relationships.** You may be thinking, "But Iuri, I'm just not very social. I don't feel like I need people. People are stupid, selfish, and judgy. I'm more of a lone-wolf kind of person." All of these things may have some truth to them, but I'm here to tell you that **you were born to connect and form deep relationships with others.** And, what's more, those relationships will be ridiculously influential in your life, and will either guarantee enormous happiness or great distress. So here is something that you MUST begin to practice in your life. You can start at home, with your parents, siblings, friends, neighbors, classmates, the person you are currently crushin' on, teachers, leaders, and so forth. Just C.A.S.H. it:

1. **C**ompliment others: "You're so nice," "Thanks for the awesome breakfast," "Nice hair (shoes, pants, style, whatever)!" "You're the best," " You're just awesome," "I love how thoughtful you are," "You look amazing today...really, every day!" Don't get all weird on me and make up some lame excuse for why you can't go and do this right away. Do it, fool!

2. **A**sk questions: Preferably about them. Start easy and surfacey, and then move a bit deeper. "What's your name?" "Do you like this teacher?" "How did you do that?" "What do you do for fun?" "What do you listen to?" "How was your day?" "How did you do on that test?" "How can you just be so cool all the time?" "Wanna go out with me?" The idea here is to show interest in the people you meet by asking them about

their lives, and what is happening in them. Oh, and if you ask, don't forget to listen.

3. **S**mile: Get out there and be a little ray of sunshine! It's simple. When you wake up in the morning, greet the people in your life with a smile. When you see your friends, smile at them. When you greet your teachers, smile at them. When you see that special someone, smile (but not in a super-freaky way). When you're walking down the hall, stand up straight, look forward, and smile. **Remember that smiling is an act of courage, and it is absolutely contagious.**

4. Offer **H**elp: It's simple, really. We all are in need of help pretty much all of the time, so you can't go wrong by offering to help your family, siblings, or friends. Here are some examples you can use right away: "Hey Mom, do you need help with something?" "Hey sista, I got your dishes, you go and get ready." "Can I take the trash out?" "Can I help with that?" "It looks like you need a bit of help—can I assist?"

CASHing it is really not that hard, and if you can awake your mind right now and commit this to memory, you'll have a simple tool that you can use from this moment forward that will give you some direction and bring some joy and friendship to yourself and those around you. Don't make excuses for not using it—do it now! Love ya.

LIFE HACK #14
WANT TO CHANGE THE WORLD?
START BY MAKING YOUR BED EVERY MORNING.

CHAPTER 15
BE UNREASONABLE

Yeah, your parents are gonna love me for this one. Listen to this terrific quote by George Bernard Shaw: "The reasonable man adapts himself to the world: the unreasonable one persists in trying to adapt the world to himself. *Therefore all progress depends on the unreasonable man.*" This quote isn't about being stupid—it's about not following the crowd, and not doing what everyone else is doing. It's about expanding, staying hungry and creative, and daring to do things differently. **The very concept of evolution depends upon the unreasonable person to not just adapt to his or her current circumstances, but to pursue creativity, learning, ideas, and an extraordinary life.** Out of the heads of such individuals will come progress, a better life and, most importantly, joy. **One of the secrets of happiness is to ensure that you are expanding and growing, and not stale and dying.**

Quick warning: by wanting to do things differently, you may discover some resistance and criticism. The greatest rebels in history (Jesus, Ghandi, and Buddha, to name a few) all discovered how unpopular and dangerous being different can be. The motto "Status quo is the way to go" is very real, and if you take an honest look around you at school and other places, you will find most people hypnotically and mindlessly doing the same things, the same way, and getting the same results. We have a tendency to get lulled to sleep in life. That's not for you! I want you to be awake and to have your eyes open! Seek for extraordinary things.

When you make choices, be a student of the consequences. Be a bit more of a scientist in the laboratory of life. Are the things you're doing building or destroying? Are you growing or atrophying? Are you promoting outstanding happiness, or misery and hurt? Come on, be unreasonable! Don't match the world or other people—have the courage to make outrageous decisions that aren't selfish, egocentric (i.e., you are the center of the world), mean, fear-based, or ignorant. **Take a shot! Push yourself! Throw away any concept or idea that says you can't do this, or do that. If you want it, take a shot—stretch yourself, your body, your mind, and your spirit, and go get it!**

You may not even realize it, but you're already infected! You're already full of habits and limiting beliefs about yourself, others, and life, which, unless you stop them, will create some havoc inside and outside of you. Here are some quick examples:

- "I'm not smart."

- "I'm not athletic."

- "I'm not a morning person."

- "I'm not brilliant or beautiful."

- "I'm just a regular dude."

- "People are dumb."

- "Math is stupid."

- "School is useless."

- "People don't change."

Your brain loves to identify quickly and to put you and others in little boxes. Recognizing that your brain does this will allow you to stay fluid, dynamic, and ripe for growing. **Think beyond your brain, for heaven's sake!**

As you step into the unknown, you may find that creativity and leadership can be lonely roads at times, but fear not—others will be there, and you may even bring some along with you. When others resist you and your efforts to change and transform, remain mind-full and steady in your resolve to grow. I'm reminded about what happens when you put crabs in a bucket and one tries to escape—the others claw at him and pull him back down. This may happen to you in life. As your friends see you growing beyond them, they may attempt to pull you back into old habits and familiar behaviors. It's a bummer when this happens. I think people do this because they don't want to lose a friend (or accomplice). In a way, we feel better and more justified when others are making the same poor decisions that we are making. As you can tell, this is not fantastic psychology. I believe that you and I can do better than this and be a bit more intelligent and deliberate about the direction our lives take.

Listen, consider what is being said, and make wise decisions. **Your ideas and dreams are valuable, and you must give them oxygen to grow.** Remember, it's less about what others are doing, or what they're not doing, and, more importantly, it's about you moving in the direction of what is extraordinary, intelligent...and yes, sometimes unreasonable and unpopular. What are you waiting for—go be massively unreasonable!

LIFE HACK #15
"IF YOU SEE GUM ON THE STREET, LEAVE IT THERE! IT'S NOT FREE CANDY."
-PAPA ELF

Chapter 16
Psychological Jiu-Jitsu
(Stop Taking Offense)

The greatest martial artist to ever live was undoubtedly Bruce Lee. His style was revolutionary and skill level legendary. He once said: "Be like water making its way through cracks. Do not resist, but adjust to the object, and you shall find a way around or through it. If nothing within you stays rigid, outward things will disclose themselves. Empty your mind, be formless. Shapeless, like water. If you put water into a cup, it becomes the cup. You put water into a bottle and it becomes the bottle. You put it in a teapot, it becomes the teapot. Now, water can flow or it can crash. Be water, my friend." What Bruce Lee was attempting to teach us is that **the great fighter is dynamic, flexible, and is able to adapt himself to any circumstance.**

The basic premise behind the Japanese martial art of Jiu-Jitsu is to use and redirect an attacker's energy back to him, instead of directly opposing it. Jiu-Jitsu is "the way of yielding," or even "the art of softness." One of our most primitive tendencies is to react, or mirror what is being offered by someone (the Bronze Rule). So, when someone is aggressive, our brain-full tendency is to reflect aggressiveness. When rudeness, insults, or accusations are thrown at us like emotional grenades, our brain-full tendency is to mirror those behaviors by being rude, insulting, or defensive in return. This internal tendency is difficult to break, but if Buddhist monks can do it after years and years of meditating in the Himalayas, then so can we (sarcasm added for your enjoyment)! **The key, of course, is to not lose your mind, but instead find it, nurture it, and answer mindfully.** Using psychological Jiu-Jitsu is a great tool to do so. What does psychological jiu-jitsu sound like?

- Them: "You're stupid!" Ninja you: "Hmm, there might be some truth to that," or "I always knew something was wrong with me," or "Yeah, but what are your thoughts about...?"

- Them: "You're a loser, and you suck at everything!" Ninja you: "Yes, I've done my share of losing, and obviously I need to do better...any suggestions?" or "Ah, you've noticed I'm not very good at this—with some time and effort, hopefully I'll do better."

- Them: "You're freaking ugly!" Ninja you: "Ugly would have been sufficient," or "Well, looks aren't everything—wouldn't you agree?" or "Opinions are like armpits, everyone's got them," or "Yeah, but I clean up really well," or "Thank you, I'll take that as a compliment."

- Them: "You're lazy!" Ninja You: "Yeah, it's not my strongest quality, huh?" or "It's true that I can be lazy—I should probably take a look at that," or "I appreciate that. How do you stay motivated?"

You get the idea. Notice how I yield to the attack—or deflect it—by agreeing with it. By doing so, I rob the the attack of its effectiveness, and whatever energy it possesses dies. That is the core principle of psychological Jiu-Jitsu, and that is why it promotes peace.

Psychological Jiu-Jitsu works because when we resist or become defensive, it adds to the problem. "What you resist...persists" is a quote I often remember and tell myself during critical discussions at work, school, and with family. This helps me to stay pliable, dynamic, and focused on what matters, instead of getting tripped up and distracted every time someone is offensive to me. I see this happen almost daily while driving. When I make a mistake driving and get honked at or flipped off, I'm quick to raise my hand and apologize to the driver, and very quickly watch their anger dissipate.

One more way of illustrating this simple concept is the folklore tale about the Oak and the Reed. In the tale, the Oak mocks the Reed because whenever a strong wind blows, the Reed seems to bend back and forth to the whim of the wind, while the Oak remains strong, upright, and

immovable. As the tale progresses, a great storm develops and the great, rigid Oak breaks, while the yielding, flexible Reed survives. The Chinese proverb, "A tree that is unbending is easily broken," is likely born from this short but wise fable.

This is really a parable about pride versus humility, insecurity versus confidence, rigidity versus flexibility, and your personal desire to be a peacemaker. You will find that this approach will help you to stay mind-full instead of getting caught up in things that are unimportant. Don Ruiz, in *The Four Agreements*, challenges us to not take anything personally. And he is not just referring to rude comments—he is referring to compliments, as well. His perspective-changing insight reveals that nothing people say to you is about you—it's really about them! Now, young Padawan, go and be like water!

Life Hack #15

"The only way to have a friend is to be one."
-Ralph Waldo Emerson

CHAPTER 17
FOUR CRAZY THINKING ERRORS

Rise and shine, buttercup! **Your psychology is everything! The way you interpret your life determines your feelings and, ultimately, your choices.** Often my job with individuals is to help them clean up their thinking and get their brains to work *for* them, instead of working against them. So, let's take a minute to look under the hood and clean up your thinking. As you already know, our brains can sometimes trick us and lead us to think and do things in ways that are not super effective or smart. **Thinking errors, or thinking distortions, are patterns of thinking that twist our perspective of life, promote fear, and keep us stuck in our problems.** In our quest to become more mind-full, conscious, and awake, it's important to become aware of some of these unconscious, mind-less practices. As you become aware of these thinking errors, you'll be able to recognize how frequently you and others mind-lessly utilize these. This is good! You cannot change something until you see it and become aware of it. That is why awareness is such a key element in being full of mind. By seeing it, you can now transform it. I'm quite familiar with all of these distortions, because I use them like candy myself (I'm working on it, all right?).

1. **Generalizing:** This thinking error assumes that something that has happened in the past will happen in the present and continue to happen in the future. Now, this can be true of some things, but not all things. Some examples of this type of thinking are: "I tried last time and failed miserably, so I'm not going to try it again." "How can I trust you—you lied to me last time!" "You always do this to me." "Teachers are lame." "People are mean and selfish." It's important that you recognize this brain tendency so that you can wisely redirect it. Your brain does this to protect you from things that have caused you harm and hurt in the past, but **the key is to**

deal with problems here and now, not then and there. Use your best thinking now to address present situations in the wisest of ways without assuming that they'll just turn out the same way as in the past.

2. **Catastrophizing:** This is one of my faves! This brain-full pattern of thinking assumes that the future will be catastrophic—that something bad is going to happen. It's a series of "What if...?" questions that lead us to feel fearful, anxious, unmotivated, and even hopeless. The brain has the brilliant capacity to imagine future events. It's something that distinguishes us from other animals, but sometimes this wonderful skill can create problems for us because it erroneously imagines the worst possible outcomes. People who struggle with anxiety and depressive symptoms often catastrophize. Here are some common examples: "This year is going to be terrible!" "No matter what I do, it's not going to work out." "I'm not going to know anyone at this party—people are going to laugh at me, and it's going to be absolutely miserable." You get the gist. You may notice that your brain has a tendency to project catastrophe. If it does, don't worry—you're just like the rest of us. When we think this way, we allow things to control our focus that may or may not happen. Your focus will result in emotions, and your emotions will likely conclude in behavior. **Don't let your catastrophic brain drive you; instead, use your mind to shift your focus to "What can I do this moment that matters and that is intelligent?"**

3. **Mind-reading:** Guess what? You are not a mind-reader! You can't look at people's faces and body language and assume you know their thoughts and intentions. I don't know why we believe that we are good this. Sure, we can take some cues from people's expressions and what they're doing, and make an educated guess about how they may be feeling or what they may be thinking, but to assume that we are right is straight up nonsense. **If you want to know about**

someone's thoughts and intentions, ask them. Give up trying to be a mind-reader—do it today! Usually, what you think people are thinking about you is a reflection of your own personal psychology, and not theirs. So, when you walk into a room and your face gets a bit red, your ears begin feeling warm, and your brain fills up with thoughts and ideas about how others are judging you, watching you, and thinking negative thoughts about you, I assure you, **you are not reading their minds, you're reading YOURS.** When your brain begins this paranoid pattern, slow it down, shift gears away from "What are people going to think?" and instead focus your energy and put it into "What can I do that would be valuable?" Sorry about ruining your life by taking away what you thought was one of your special extra-terrestrial abilities.

4. **Stop comparing:** Probably the most common thinking error youth engage in is comparison. Comparison is the brain-full pattern of measuring. Imagine walking around constantly comparing ourselves, our lives, our looks, and our intelligence to others. When we do this, we are usually measuring the worst about ourselves against what we believe is the best about others...yeah, this will leave you feeling worthless and like a failure. **You know you're caught up in this psychological trap if you experience jealousy or feel worse about yourself when others do well.** Don't worry—I believe we've all experienced this kind of poor psychology, but today you can begin to change that by stopping the madness, and deciding to stop comparing yourself to others in life.

Remember that your brain is a tool. It's not perfect. Our job is to interact with it—make it run a little cleaner, a little more accurately and, as a result, have it become a better instrument for you happiness.

Life Hack #17
Pay for the person in line behind you.

Chapter 18
Your Happiness Toolbox

Yo, I'm about to throw down some advice and information your way that you are going to want to listen to. Without a doubt, "I want to be a happier" is the most common request or treatment goal that I hear from clients. People want their lives to be full of joy, excitement, and newness; in other words, they want to feel alive, not just be alive. Guess what? I want that for you, too (despite what I said in Chapter 13). But we cannot think of happiness just as a feeling or destination; rather, it is a state of being joyful. **Being and feeling joyful is a way of thinking about and relating to the world, others, and yourself. Being joyful is about noticing the light in the world around you, in others, and in yourself. It's peace, thankfulness, and hope wrapped up in one. It's a wonderful confidence that this life is for you, and that the experiences you have and will go through will build you and make you wiser and more valuable. Joy is unreasonable! It has little to do with the external state of things, and everything to do with your internal state.** So, enough of my chatter let's get down to the nitty-gritty about how to raise the levels of joy in your life. The first five suggestions come from the writings of Martin Seligman and his research on happiness and well-being. The remainder are mine, but they'll soon become yours.

- **Increase positive feelings in your life:** People who are happier do more things that create feelings of happiness, excitement, and laughter in their lives. "Congratulations, Sherlock!" Okay, don't get all huffy with me, but think about it. **If you want to increase your levels of joy in life, you must engage in things that create those feelings inside you.** Do you know what those things are for you? If you want to improve your happiness, what do you do? Why don't you make a list of 10, or 20, or 100 things you know will give you a little boost, and then get to work sprinkling those things into your life on a more consistent basis.

- **Engage:** People who experience higher levels of joy in their lives are engaged in things they believe are meaningful and worthwhile. We have a rule in our house: you have to be involved in something while you're in school. I don't care what it is, but you have to choose something that you can sink your focus and attention into that will stretch you and help you grow. If you're not doing that right now, make an immediate plan to start right away. It could be an instrument, a club, a sport, drawing, writing, theater, singing, a new skill or hobby, or something else. But it has to engage you, meaning, you have to lose yourself in it! "But Iuri, I don't know what I like; I don't know what my passion is!" It's okay, you big whiner, just begin! Part of your purpose in life is exploring and discovering. Engage in different things. Really put some solid effort in excelling at something, and that something may become a passion, or it might not. Either way, it's a win-win. When you pursue something great, even if it isn't your favorite thing, you add to yourself depth and a richer experience of the world around you. It helps you to see things through different eyes and makes you more compassionate and understanding of those whom you've gotten to know on a personal level. It's worth it—trust me. Now, get your booty off your couch, and go engage!

- **Positive Relationships:** People who are happier have positive relationships. They surround themselves with people who are positive, inspiring, encouraging, and loving. Whether you are at church, work, school, or in your neighborhood, begin gravitating toward these people, and become friendly toward them. It's important for you to become this kind of individual yourself, so start there, and then place yourself at the right spot, surround yourself with lovely people, and reap a lifetime of benefits from having people around you who are uplifting.

- **Meaningful:** Listen—not all activities and things you do are meaningful. **Things in life carry a different weight of importance and meaning. Your job is to engage in those things that carry the most value and importance.** For example, watching Netflix is lower on the scale of value than playing an instrument. One is stagnant, the other requires effort, engagement, and is the very act of evolution. Meaningful things train your mind and body to evolve. They force the mind, body, and soul to expand. **Being wise in this life has a great deal to do with your choices to pursue and invest your time in things that are of the greatest importance**, while placing to the side those things that are detrimental and less important. Be smart, and stick to meaningful things.

- **Achievement:** Happy people find ways to create achievement in their life. They run races, climb mountains, perform, set goals, learn a new song—they spend time improving. This feeling of achieving, finishing, or getting better at something is important to your emotional and psychological well-being. Become engaged in things that help you experience the rewards of achievement.

- **Creativity and expansion:** I constantly tell people, your life needs some movement—it needs expansion and evolution. We must expand as individuals, because that is who we are and what we are meant to be. **Arouse your faculties and engage in creative pursuits that awake and stretch your brain, body, and spirit. To be absolutely clear and honest, you cannot be happy and stagnant at the same time.** This doesn't mean that you need to be rushing around, busy all the time—it just means that you must invest in things that build you in order for you to experience more and more moments of joy.

- **Exercise thankfulness:** Having an attitude of gratitude is good solid advice if you are looking to create some joy in your life. **Being grateful to the people around you, in addition to noticing the beauty around you and in others, naturally fosters and creates happiness.** Most religious practices involve prayer and meditation, which are both vehicles that drive you to notice and express gratitude. If you don't do either of those (get busy doing it—why not?), start a gratitude journal on your phone and simply complete the following sentence: "Today I'm grateful for _____." And then expound a bit as to why you are grateful for those things. **You can live in a state of contentment and joy if you can educate your eyes and mind to capture the beauty that is constantly happening inside and outside of you.** If your life is full of complaining, grumbling, noticing what you don't have, comparing with others, feeling like you're missing out— welcome to misery. Do yourself a favor and begin to do this today and forever.

- **Promote goodwill:** Now that you have read Chapter 10, you know that you are constantly promoting one thing or another in your life. In the past 14 years of listening to the most private details, thoughts, and desires of people from every walk of life, it has become perfectly clear to me that **people who experience the highest levels of happiness, joy, and peace are constantly promoting goodwill in their personal and interpersonal relationships.** These people have figured out the simple truth that **it is more valuable to give than to receive.** As you decide today to be a giver and not a taker, you will begin to promote goodness, compassion, kindness, consideration for others, patience, and friendliness. Remember that your brain is a tool that will learn what you repeatedly ask it to do. So, teach your brain to not only notice the beautiful things of life, but also to promote them in yourself and others. Here are some simple things you can do right now:

a. Smile at people.

b. Remember people's names.

c. Forgive people for their mistakes.

d. Give people high-fives and congratulate them.

e. Compliment people.

f. Ask people questions about their lives.

g. Greet your family members in the morning and always say goodnight to them when you go to sleep.

h. Say please and thank you.

i. Laugh often and add humor to the world around you.

- **Know that all things can be consecrated for your good:** This extraordinary psychology is an absolute necessity for this life. To consecrate something means to make it holy and important. As you already know, life is full of unfairness, injustice, rudeness, pain, suffering, etc., yet this simple, beautiful, and true pearl of wisdom will allow you to experience all of the harshness that life has to offer with an enlightened perspective. **That perspective, of course, is that all things can be had for our good, and to enhance our experience.** I know that some of you have already experienced horrible things, and I truly wish you hadn't. I feel a great sense of compassion for you, yet I know and believe in my heart that you can transform these difficult experiences into powerful and valuable knowledge. Please believe me, because it is absolutely true. **Remember that the power to assign meaning to your life rests within you. Either your brain assigns a meaning by default, or you deliberately and mind-fully decide what your life will mean.** This is the beautiful ability to be in the world, but not of the world. Best of luck, my friend.

- **Practice mind-fullness:** One of the purposes of this book is to open your eyes and awaken you from robotic and unconscious patterns that aren't that great, and instead have you become aware of the fullness of life that can be achieved as you live purposefully and mind-fully. As you now know, to be mind-full is to observe and respond with purpose. To be brain-full is to be caught up and reactive. Being mind-full is knowing that you can bring joy, peace, goodwill, humor, fun, and friendship to any circumstance, or, conversely, that you can provoke anger, bitterness, gossip, hurt, and pain to any circumstance. **To be mind-full is to enter each moment with curiosity and the knowledge that we can influence every event and circumstance in our lives.** When one is mind-full and awake, divine beauty in the grandest or simplest of things becomes manifest, and we naturally develop a thankful heart and mind.

I want you to **realize that happiness is the ultimate discipline.** In Dan Millman's *Way of The Peaceful Warrior: A Book That Changes Lives*, we learn that "**A fool is happy when his cravings are satisfied. A warrior is happy for no reason.**" Become familiar with the suggestions I've shared above, and begin to find ways to implement them in your life. I wish you a life full of meaning, peace, love, and joy. Now, go and get it.

LIFE HACK #18
"TO LIVE IS THE RAREST THING IN THE WORLD.
MOST PEOPLE EXIST, THAT'S ALL."
-OSCAR WILDE

CHAPTER 19
PEOPLE, PLACES & THINGS

G'day, mate! Hope you are having a lovely day. Let's add to your already amazing knowledge by introducing a quick and easy saying that has helped many a person. Sometimes in life, people develop extremely powerful addictions to alcohol, cigarettes, drugs, and other things. You may know individuals who have become entangled in that miserable web—some may even be your relatives. I love these people. I have worked with them, cried with them, and have seen many emancipate themselves from a life of slavery. Every time I see someone succeed, I feel like it's a miracle. It's a miracle because these people don't just have to stop drinking or doing drugs—they often have to transform their psychology, their social settings, realign their spirituality, and at times straight-up move to a different place. Like I said, their efforts are amazing!

"People, places, and things" is a reference to that transformation. **If you want to successfully improve or transform something in your life, know that you will likely have to change the people you're with, the places you frequent, and the things that you talk about and do.** I know what you're thinking: "Iuri, my friend, my mom and dad have already told me to pick good friends, blah, blah, blah..." Bro! Sista! I'm not here to tell you what to do or what not to do—I'm here to tell you that if you want to succeed and become extraordinary at something, frequent the places, be with the people, and do the things that extraordinary people do, period! Want to become a musician? Begin to make friends with other musicians, and jam with them. You'll find that their talents will enhance your own style. Want to be happier? Hang out with people who do life right, are loyal, friendly, do exciting things, and love to laugh. Want to increase your spirituality? Place yourself in holy places, with people who are believers, and who want to better their spirituality. Want to be a great student? Get your little rear end up and plant it in the first or second row in class, and get together for study groups with people who do well in those classes. Want to be better at a specific sport? Spend time with people who are good at that sport, and play it often. This makes sense, right?

The principle also works if you are trying to stop doing something that has caused you some personal, family, or legal problems. This includes things like alcohol, pornography, drugs, stealing, fighting, gossiping, and vaping, among other things. I'm telling you this so that you can avoid the common mental trap that I repeatedly hear from some of my clients, which sounds something like this: "Iuri, I can just stop if I want to." "It's my choice, not theirs, whether I do it or not." "I'm strong enough to say no—I've done it before." "My friends will respect my choice; they won't push me to do something I don't want to do." "I don't have to change everything in my life just to stop." I hope you know that I love you and respect your efforts to live and choose your life. It's truly your journey, my friend, and I want you to "live deep, and suck the marrow," and to do that, at some point, you've got to speak and believe the truth. **If you are thinking along the lines of those statements I have mentioned, you're not in the real world, you don't truly know others, and you certainly don't know yourself.**

I'm reminded of Peter, one of Christ's disciples. At the end of Jesus' life, He met with His apostles and told them that by the end of the night all of them would forsake and become ashamed of Him. I'm sure this was disturbing news to these men who had followed Jesus and watched him do miraculous and amazing things. Peter spoke up and emphatically said, "Lord, I will never leave thee!" Jesus gently asserted that Peter would not only leave Him, but would also deny Him three times, all before the rooster heralded a new day. Soon after, a posse of people came and arrested Jesus and took him to be tried. Peter followed Jesus and found himself in the chief priest's palace. While there, someone accused him of being one of Jesus' disciples. Peter denied it. Moments later, another suggested that Peter knew Christ. Again, Peter denied it. A third time someone accused him, and Peter stated, "I know not the man!" Immediately the rooster crowed. At that moment, Peter's eyes met Christ's, and

Peter wept bitterly. I have no ill judgment of Peter. He was brave, outspoken, and proved himself to be loyal and stalwart, yet in this situation none of that mattered, all because he was in the wrong place and with the wrong people and, as a result, he betrayed himself and Christ.

The wonderful moral for you is this: **Stay out of the places that make it hard for you to be true to yourself. In other words, if you want to stop drinking, stop going to the bar. If you want to stop smoking pot, stop hanging around pot-smokers. It's just intelligent, and I know that you want to be intelligent.** So take this little pebble of wisdom, and plant it inside your brain. Best of luck.

LIFE HACK #19
"ONLY A LIFE LIVED FOR OTHERS IS A LIFE WORTHWHILE."
-ALBERT EINSTEIN

Chapter 20
Watch Your Language

Listen up—the words that exit your mouth matter, not only to the people around you, but also to yourself. **Our words are like spells that can encourage, promote love, invite peace, motivate, inspire, and create hope. The opposite is also true: they can destroy, provoke anger, cause pain, dash hopes, and promote ignorance and hatred.** This is what you need to know—you are in control! **You are the author of the influence you are constantly sowing.** You've probably heard people say, "I didn't mean to say that." I believe them—people are unconscious so much of their lives, that half the time they are not fully conscious of the words that are coming out of their mouths. As I've previously stated, the goal of the enlightened person is to awake and to consciously live his or her life. Hopefully this small chapter will prompt you to watch your language and become aware of the words that come out of your mouth when you speak to your sister, brother, mother, father, friends, and others around you. Do your words inspire friendship—or division? Do they promote kindness—or rudeness? Do they they invite freedom—or fear?

Words are how we describe and interpret the world around us. The tales you tell yourself have a dramatic impact on how you think and feel. Of course we can all joke and have fun with each other, but there are times when the words we speak literally bind us and create a kind of self-fulfilling prophecy. Here are some things I hear people convincing themselves of, and some tips on how to speak more truthfully (in parentheses):

- "I'm no good at science." ("Not yet, but with a little bit of patience, effort, and help, I can improve.")

- "I'm not a morning person." ("My brain will do whatever I teach it to do.")

- "I'm not good at sports." ("I can improve at whatever activity I persistently practice and engage in.")

- "I'm just not that smart." ("Not yet, perhaps, but little by little my brain will expand, grow, learn, and become more intelligent. Hang in there, Einstein!")

- "People are stupid." ("Some people may have moments of stupidity and ignorance. Some are more mind-full than others. I like to give people the benefit of the doubt. Also, remember that I am a person, too.")

- "School's just not for me!" ("School can be very tough—I may need help from time to time. Asking for help is intelligent.")

- "I'm ugly, gross, fat, skinny..." ("I will become loyal to myself, starting today. I will not speak in demeaning ways about myself or about others. If there are things to improve upon, I won't jump into a pity party—I'll get busy doing something about it.")

- "I'm just not as good as so-and-so. ("That may be true, but I can get better at anything I choose to focus on.")

- "My parents don't know anything." ("They don't know everything, but they do know some things. They have lived on this planet for over a century!")

- "Life's not fair." Actually, you're right about that one.

- "I hate my life." ("I seriously dislike some moments in my life, but I also really like a lot of moments in my life. More importantly, I can do something about it.")

Saying these words to your brain is like playing fetch with a dog. Throw the ball, and there goes the dog (brain). Tell your brain these things, and not only will your brain begin to believe them, but it will also go and find the evidence to confirm that they are true (remember confirmation bias in Chapter 17).

So, what's my advice to you? **Never put yourself or others into boxes, especially negative ones.** Quit making such definitive and debilitating statements about what you are, and what you think you will be forever and ever! Some of these statements can be altered by simply ending them with the word YET, others can be improved as you seek to soften the judgements they make about yourself, others, and the world. Look, this isn't me just blowing hot air, or ignorantly telling you, "You can do whatever you want in life— you can be and do anything you want...blah, blah, blah," because the reality is that you probably can't do everything, but man or woman, **you can improve, expand, and become better at just about anything you wish in this life. Your brain, mind, body, and soul are made to do this! There is no arguing this point, so quit limiting yourself by filling your brain and other people's brains with lies and self-limiting beliefs, 'capiche'?**

So, awake and arise, my friend! Whether directed at yourself or others, become aware of the words that are filling up your brain and pouring from your mouth. You may find that it is dramatically more difficult to do this when you are angry, fearful, resentful, tired, hungry, or caught up in some self-victim place. It's at those times that you'll have to use the mind to master the brain and speak consciously instead of carelessly. This is a vital skill; every one of your relationships will depend upon your ability to master the art of speaking mind-fully rather than mindlessly. Now, go and be absolutely brilliant!

LIFE HACK #20

"SPREAD LOVE EVERYWHERE YOU GO. LET NO ONE EVER COME TO YOU WITHOUT LEAVING HAPPIER."
- MOTHER TERESA

Chapter 21
Ask for Help, for Heaven's Sake!

I hope your day is going great and that you are shining bright! In your quest for amazing amounts of fun, wisdom, joy, and enlightenment, you will likely struggle mightily and fail miserably. Yay, welcome the losers' club! I'm a part of it, so I promise you won't be alone. This is a reality! You don't know everything, and you will never know everything. Some things will be easy for you, and some will be very difficult. The problem is that sometimes we are so doggone hard-headed, aren't we? We will fail, get behind, and just become completely lost and not ask for help. Why don't we ask for help more often? Why don't you ask for help? Here are some reasons I often hear:

- "I don't want to bother people with my problems."
- "I got it, I can figure it out" (sometimes this is true).
- "I don't want to sound stupid."
- "This isn't that important."
- "I don't want other people to think I need help."
- "Asking for help won't help. It didn't in the past."
- "I'm embarrassed that I'm not doing well and I don't want others to know."

Now, we are people seeking for enlightenment, are we not? We seek for the good things—to be wise, to excel, and to grow beyond our bounds. This whole "Help is for the birds" thing ends today. **The wise seeker of wisdom must be humble. Pride and fear are the wall that keep us from being open to the truth and the wisdom that rests outside of it.** Admit today (or tomorrow, if you wish) that sometimes things aren't going to go well, and that you can ask for and accept help.

Ask yourself this question: "Is it more mature to seek and accept help, or to pretend that everything is fine, not ask for help, and not accept help from others?" Look, there's no weird judgment from me—I know what it's like to not answer a question correctly. I know what it's like to sit in class not knowing what people are talking about, and not raising my hand to ask a question. I know what it's like to fail a class, and to be so completely lost in it to the point that you stop going. My own fear of embarrassment prevented me from doing the simplest of things, which was to just ask for help. To simply say, "Mom, Dad, I'm not doing well in math—I think I need some help." I mean, would that just be horrible?

I want your rational mind to hear me right now. If you are struggling, failing, or not succeeding at something that matters in your life, will you please just find someone that gives a hoot, and ask for help already? I know your fearful brain is going to town right now, saying, "Yeah, but Iuri, my situation is different...blah, blah, blah." I hear you, I hear you. I'm not saying you can't do things on your own—go for it, keep giving it a go! But let's keep it real. If you are truly not doing well, it's time for you to evolve beyond the culture of fear, pride, insecurity, and embarrassment, and move into a culture of confidence, humility, and courage. Let's do it together!

As a parent, teacher, friend, and therapist, some of the most amazing words I ever hear are: "Iuri, what do you think I should do about...?" or "Things aren't going well—can you help me with...?" or "I need a little help, do you have a moment?" or "Dad, can you help me?" Oh man, I feel so honored to help, and so proud of the individual who is willing to seek that help. Just think about it. If this idea makes sense to you, then perhaps you can begin to make a small adjustment in your life, and take advantage of some of the resources that are around you, instead of being paralyzed by your fears and insecurities. Now, go and do!

Life Hack #21
"Everything has beauty, but not everyone sees it."
-Confucius

Chapter 22
Day by day, Hour by Hour, Moment by Moment

No two moments are ever the same. No matter how much it may seem that way, each moment is unique and carries within it the seeds for something different—for something new. I want you to become a moment-by-moment person. When life is happening around you, I want you to be fully present. That means here, now, awake, mind-full, and deliberately doing what is wise.

It's obvious that we are not perfect. Oftentimes we make serious mistakes—things that will hang over us, burden us, and drag us down. **The past can sometimes cast a long shadow, become a heavy burden, and kill our motivation. Often times this happens because we are secretly holding onto things that we are ashamed of, or because we have left unfortunate circumstances in the past unresolved. Sometimes the past will continue to haunt us because we assume that things will remain the same, that we will fail despite our best efforts, and that we and others cannot change. This is a lie! It logically cannot be true!** To believe it would be to give up our power and ability to transform every moment. No matter how much we may try to kill our own power with negative talk, we cannot. The truth that **we are a power unto ourselves** will always return in those simple moments of clarity and truth. I'm here now to rekindle that power, and to help you build it.

So many times people come to me because they are trying to stop doing something they are embarrassed about, or something they want to stop because it's causing difficulties in their lives. As is often the case, they try to change their behavior, but they fail here and there. These failures (5% to 10% of the time) seem to somehow carry more influence and power than the successes (90% to 95%) they achieve. How does this happen? I mean, I'm no freaking mathematician, but this just doesn't compute. **We are so quick to** let our failures define who we are, and so slow to let our **positive efforts, righteous desires, and successes define who we are instead. Why is that? I think it's because we believe that the bad that people do, matters more than the good they do.** Apparently we value it more, because newspapers and news are filled with what is going wrong with the world, and we love it. I'm not suggesting we don't pay attention to those things. If you're trying to stop looking at pornography, or drinking, or using drugs, or having sex, or masturbating, or stealing, or cheating, you should definitely address those things and engage them in a way that helps you overcome the things that can and will pollute your body, mind, and spirit. I just don't want every mistake to make you feel like you're a failure and like you have to start from the very begining, because that just isn't true. Pick up from where you are and go forward, you silly little freak! **Our mistakes reveal things to us—be brave enough to look at them; learn from them; ask for help when needed; and let's get back on the rock** (see Chapter 26 - What Climbing Has Taught Me). **Remember to not let your imperfect past derail your perfect beginnings.** Others may remember and may judge your past mistakes and weaknesses. There is nothing we can do about that—actually, the only thing we can do is boldly and bravely begin again, wiser, more experienced, and better able to improve. I believe it, and you'd better believe it too.

LIFE HACK #22

"NOTHING WILL WORK UNLESS YOU DO."
-MAYA ANGELOU

Chapter 23
People Have the Right to Suffer

"Wow, Iuri, this chapter sounds super fun—I can't wait to read it!" I'm glad you're excited, because this concept is crucial for you to understand. Viktor Frankl, who was a prisoner in a Nazi concentration camp, stated, "If there is any meaning in life, then there must be meaning in suffering." Why? Well, for one, because there is so much of it. I'm certain you've experienced it, and it won't be the last time. Pain can be a frightening companion, yet it can be a most effective teacher and motivator. I'm not suggesting that we go around causing hurt and pain to others, or that we don't comfort others in their moments of pain and disappointment. And yet, I don't know if we need to rescue everyone from their suffering, either.

So often I hear, "Well, I just don't want to hurt their feelings," or "I don't want them to feel bad." Why? Why can't we feel bad? The truest answer to that question is: we can feel bad! We can feel pain! And more importantly, that pain can teach us and provide us with deep meaning in life. Our own personal fear of failure is similar to this idea. You may not try different and difficult things for fear that you will fail and thus suffer. **You and I have become too afraid to suffer and, as a result, we have become prisoners of what is comfortable, familiar, and easy. The crazy truth is that in the end our fear of suffering will cause us more of it.**

I remember a while back when a friend called me asking me whether she should bail her husband out of jail for something he had done. I told her "absolutely not." Not because I was looking to punish him, or because I was trying to make him feel horrible for what he had done. I just didn't think she needed to intervene and get in the way of what I believe was an immensely important opportunity for him. My great hope for him, of course, was that the pain of his situation could in some way awaken him, as it had awakened me at specific times in my life. So, when people are suffering for things that they have done, listen to them, be understanding of them—but don't necessarily rescue them. Allow them the right to suffer and, as a result, reap the benefits of their suffering.

I sometimes hear of boys and girls who stay in super unhealthy relationships for fear of hurting their boyfriend or girlfriend's feelings. **I've heard of boys and girls who put up with and do things that go against their personal morals (sex, sexting, sending nude pictures, cheating, stealing, lying, putting up with abusive behavior) because they didn't want to hurt someone. This cannot happen to you anymore! If your boyfriend or girlfriend threatens to commit suicide or hurt themselves if you break up, it's time to break up, and let someone who can help know what has been said.** I'm not suggesting that those situations are easy—I'm just letting you know what the mind-full, confident, and enlightened individual will do, and hoping that you will have the courage to do it, as well.

LIFE HACK #23
IN A WORLD WHERE YOU CAN BE ANYTHING, BE KIND.

Chapter 24
You're Never Standing Still

Time to shake what yo' momma gave you! Check this out—I'm about to show you a universal law: **Whatever you invest in expands, and whatever you neglect atrophies. In other words, whatever you focus and give energy to, grows. Whatever you focus away from becomes smaller.** This is true physically, intellectually, spiritually, and socially. When you focus on and invest in running, swimming, or lifting weights, you always grow in those areas. When you invest in practicing an instrument, you naturally expand in your ability to play that instrument. Whenever you spend time investing in your relationships with people or God, those relationships expand. Whenever you neglect your relationships, they become less significant and more distant. This is fantastic knowledge! **It means that your brain and body become a literal representation of your physical, spiritual, psychological, and intellectual investments. Isn't that terrifyingly awesome?!**

Two things that are important to ask yourself here:

1. What am I currently investing in?

2. What do I want to invest in?

Regardless of what your answer is to those specific questions, it's important for you to recognize that **you are never standing still. Your body, mind, and spirit are never stagnant—they are always moving either toward growth or atrophy. Your muscles don't maintain—they are either in a state of growth or decline. Your relationships are the same. They are either becoming stronger and closer, or they are becoming irrelevant.**

There is an old Native American parable that reflects this teaching. The parable suggests that inside each of us are two wolves— a good wolf and a bad one. When you feed one it grows bigger and more influential in your life; conversely, the other starves and becomes inconsequential. **Make sure you are feeding the right wolf.**

A big part of this simple and critical chapter is to help you realize that you are always consciously or unconsciously investing in being stronger, more resilient, more understanding, more loving, or more courageous; or investing in only doing the easy things, or being weaker, more judgmental, more unkind, and more driven by fear. I'm hopeful that, as you take a look at your relationships with your parents, siblings, and friends, you will choose to invest more kindly and wisely. As you examine your studies, your involvement in sports, your spirituality, and your other skills (art, music, writing, etc), be wise and invest in those things that will provide the most meaning, and that are of greater importance. So come on, and shake what yo' momma gave you!

LIFE HACK #24
PICK AND DO 3 IMPORTANT THINGS EACH DAY— THAT'S 1,095 WORTHWHILE THINGS EACH YEAR.

Chapter 25
Decisions, not Conditions

I hope you're awake, 'cause you're about to get a shot of reality! Tony Robbins, a very successful motivational speaker, once said, "It's your decisions, not your conditions, that determine your destiny." Think about that statement and add this one to it by Thomas S. Monson: "It has been said that the door of history turns on small hinges, and so do people's lives. The choices we make determine our destiny." As a therapist and social scientist for over 15 years, I've literally listened to the intimate details of thousands of people's lives. As a result, I've come to realize the truth of these two statements. In summary, **your decisions *now* matter more than your circumstances *then*.** I'm not attempting to scare you—I'm telling you this for two reasons:

1. I want you to awake and begin to consciously make decisions that are wise, and that fill your life with rich talents, habits, and opportunities.

2. I want you to know, with absolute certainty, that at any point you can realign your future by making better and wiser decisions today.

I've met people at these crossroads before. They've come into my office in massive amounts of pain. Their life decisions have led them to jail, dead-ends, divorce, addiction, dropping out of high school, legal issues, broken relationships, and deep regrets. As I've sat and listened to their stories and their choices over the years, it's easy to see the icebergs that these individuals were unconsciously headed toward. "Hindsight is 20/20," it's been said, and in my own life, and in other people's lives, that seems to be true as well. I often say, no one ever starts smoking weed, drinking, or using other drugs to end up on skidrow, or in a jail cell, or with a massive physical, psychological, and emotional addiction, or passed out with a needle in their arm, and yet...and yet, a significantly high number of the people who make those seemingly small choices at very young ages end up there!

We don't always control our conditions. We're placed here in a variety of cultural, familial, emotional, and psychological conditions. Some situations can be filled with enormous challenge and tragedy, while others are more fortunate. Life is certainly not fair, and perhaps one day we will further understand the reason for those great discrepancies, but for now the individual truth for you remains—**you can make decisions now! Make them today, tomorrow, and the next day:**

- Decide to make peace, not war, with the people around you.

- Study, learn, graduate, and pursue higher education degrees and certifications. Become excellent at many things.

- Engage yourself in physical activities, sports, artistic pursuits, social events, and spiritual environments that stretch you and motivate you to grow.

- Seek for kind, inspiring, loyal, and honest friends...become one yourself first.

- Become more honorable in your actions toward yourself and others.

- Stop complaining, and start working through problems and looking for solutions.

- Don't ever speak ill of anyone.

- Forgive those who have hurt you.

- Own your stuff, apologize, make reparations, and move on!

- Learn to love others by being loving to them.

- Be patient and compassionate with yourself and others.

- Remember that you get credit for trying, and trying, and trying again.

I don't know you (or do I?), or where you came from, or where you're going, but I'm absolutely hopeful and confident that you can bravely decide to live your life with your eyes wide open, and make decisions that are more directly aligned with brilliance! It's never too late, and it's never too early! Your decisions mattered yesterday, and they will matter today and tomorrow. Don't limit yourself in what you can and can't do! Don't give up something that is worthwhile because it's hard! Begin shaping a great and joyous life today by making the kinds of choices that will help you arrive there. Good luck, and see you on the path!

LIFE HACK #25
"DON'T RAISE YOUR VOICE, IMPROVE YOUR ARGUMENT."
-DESMOND TUTU

CHAPTER 26
WHAT CLIMBING HAS TAUGHT ME

Check it out! I've been rock climbing now for over a decade. It's been a really exciting addition to my life. I remember growing up in the southern coast of Portugal, scrambling up and down rocks and cliffsides to reach the most spectacular, beautiful, and secluded beaches in that part of the land. Those early beginnings became a passion once I was introduced to rock climbing in my 20's by a good friend. I simply had to do it! It was exciting, challenging, but most of all, very cool! Climbing has not only become a fun hobby, and something I share with my family and friends, but it's also become an integral part of my therapy business. I call it Adventure-Based Therapy. I climb, boulder, rappel, and take people on canyoneering trips as a magnificent tool to help them grow, expand, overcome their fears, and heal. I believe it is the best form of therapy!

The moment I began climbing, I started noticing the link in my mind between this extreme sport and therapy. I think they fit together quite nicely. The elements of trust, focus, mind-fullness, skill-building, strength, finesse, planning, managing risk, and lots of fun, seemed perfect to add to my therapeutic approach. So, without further ado, here are the top 10 things I've learned from climbing:

1. **Climbing is a matter of time, effort, and experience:** I've introduced climbing to thousands of people. Even though I believe that we are all meant and made to climb, climbing is hard, scary, and oftentimes frustrating. People constantly tell me, "Iuri, you make it look so easy." My response is always the same: "The only difference between you and I is a little bit of time and experience." Once people take the time to learn how to hang on the rock, build their calluses, strengthen their muscles, and focus their minds, climbing will become "seemingly effortless" for them also. You will find that there is a direct application to this simple

truth in your life. Weather it's statistics, piano, soccer, art, writing, kissing (I know...even that), meditating, praying, singing, driving, developing social courage, skiing, skateboarding—**nothing is out of your reach. It's all a matter of time, effort, and experience, know what I'm sayin'??**

2. **Fall with style:** Falling is an essential part of climbing. It's so important that I'll often spend hours teaching people how to fall correctly. As you become better and better at climbing, you will begin to expose yourself to more difficult climbs, thus increasing your risk of falling. All falling is managed in climbing, and with a little bit of focus and intelligence, it's safer than walking to school. I equate falling with failing. When teaching this principle I often quote the words of Winston Churchill, who said, **"Failure is not fatal, success is not final."** Climbers will often cheer and compliment a nice fall. It's not uncommon to hear climbers say, "Wow, that was a really gnarly fall...well done!" Climbers are all a little sick in the head, yet the idea that falling (or failing) is natural, even something we practice and become better at, is a really cool concept. So, what happens when you fall? Well, you simply pull yourself together, chalk up your hands, plan a little bit, and climb again! That's how you fall with style. So when you fall in life, remember Buzz Lightyear, and fall with style.

3. **You can learn to focus your thinking, and manage your emotions:** Climbing is a physically strenuous sport, and an emotionally charged activity. Fear is natural in climbing. Most brains will experience fear at high altitudes, with the possibility of falling to one's death. This is real! And yet, climbing, when done right, is meant to be done in a very conscious and relaxed way. So, how do we make our body relax, when our brain is sounding the alarm? **You learn to manage the brain by learning how to mind-fully focus on the things you can manage and that matter in that instant.** In climbing this usually means: slowing

your breathing, focusing on planting your feet on the rock, not squeezing the rock tighter than you need to, and keeping your arms long and relaxed. By doing these things, you can mind-fully communicate back to your brain, and calm it down. Summary: **Slow yourself down, focus on the things you can control and that matter, act on them, and repeat!**

4. **Some things have to be perfect:** The wise friend who taught me to climb told me once, "Iuri, in climbing, you've got one good mistake in you, and then you die." That's the deal! I'm no nihilist, and I'm certainly not looking to die, so when it comes to certain parts of climbing, I have to be fully conscious and be perfect, no matter how many times I've done something. I'm thinking specifically of the knots I tie, the way I attach a harness to the rope with a carabiner, the equipment I use—you get the idea. When I'm teaching people how to climb, I often teach them that concept—that in certain areas of their lives, they have to be fully alert, fully conscious, and perform at their highest level, because the consequences are just too great. As your friend, let me suggest three areas for you to be perfect at: (1) Make drugs and alcohol off limits for you. Seriously, I don't care how you paint it, justify it, what's legal or not, let's let common sense, reason, and intelligence save you from this obvious trap. (2) Sex. Wait 'til you are married to engage in this sacred and intimate act. I don't care about what media, movies, songs, or magazines say, or what you're friends are doing—the consequences and the value that is inherent in this sacred act of commitment are too great for you to squander willy-nilly. (3)Pornography. Don't view it, don't share it, don't ask for it, don't participate in it. Boys, never, ever, ever, no—never—ask girls for nudes or inappropriate pictures. This is unkind and super uncool. Girls, if a boy ever asks you for those...? Bye-bye, that boy is not for you! I don't care if they are hot, cool, lonely, suicidal, questioning the relationship, or pressuring—it's a no-go! Anyway, think it through, I love you!

5. **It matters who is belaying you:** When I introduce people to climbing, I usually have them belay me while I climb up to set up a route. The large majority of individuals have never belayed before. I teach them, trust them and the gear, and I climb on. Most of the people that I climb with are beginners, but every once in awhile, I'll climb with people who are experienced, fully focused, and encouraging. This matters; in fact, it matters a lot, and influences the level of confidence that I have while climbing. In life it is the same. Who's got you in life? Your family? Your friends? Your neighbors? When you find someone who is an awesome "belayer" in life, **someone who is encouraging, positive, looks out for your best interest, and helps you to feel confident, stay close to him or her because a good friend is worth more than rubies.**

6. **Give and take "beta" in life:** Most climbing is done socially, meaning you need more than yourself to climb. Climbers love to talk about climbing and give each other bits of "beta"—or information—about a certain climb. This can happen before the climb, during it, or after. We want people to reach the top and to succeed. I've climbed with people who do not take "beta" very well. They are not open or attentive to the "beta" that I give them. They are climbing on their own. No worries—there's no negative judgment here, I enjoy the challenge of discovering a route on my own as well, yet when someone is trying to help you, be humble and wise enough to keep your heart open, soft, and willing. **Humility is a trademark of individuals who are not only enlightened, but who are on the path to enlightenment and joy.** So in life, give and receive beta.

7. **Some things don't need to be held onto so hard:** Climbing is seemingly simple and straightforward, yet there are these tiny little tricks and skills in climbing that make the experience more successful. One of these is learning to only squeeze the rock as hard as you need to, and no more. Often, people who are just beginning to climb grip the rock as if

their life depends on it. I call it the death grip. The reality is that most holds don't require a death grip, they simply need a relaxed grip. Learning when to grip and pinch the rock extremely hard, and when not to, is an essential key to climbing effectively, and not getting completely exhausted. Similarly, I find that **people in life hold on to things that have very little value with a death grip. We hold on to people who are unhealthy to us, to behavior that is scandalous or unwise, and to certain ideas and beliefs that are just plain unintelligent. Why do we become so loyal to things that have so little value?** Some examples are: video games, people who are hurtful to us, TV, phones, marijuana, pornography, laziness, limiting and negative beliefs about ourselves and others, drama and gossip, music, etc. The point is, hold on tooth and nail to the things that carry the most value and importance in life, and ease your grip on the unimportant things in your life.

8. **See it, think it, climb it:** When I first introduce people to climbing, I teach them to see the climb from beginning to end, to think through the climb (create a basic mental strategy) and, once their feet and hands are on the rock, it's time to move and climb it! When they or I fall, the pattern restarts. See it, think it, climb it. Often, people get on the rock without looking at where they're going, and without any plan. **I teach them to slow it down a bit and add a little thought to what they're doing. I teach them to climb deliberately instead of accidentally.** This sounds like a good way to live a life, don't you think? Let's aim where we're headed, make a plan that's dynamic, get our hands and feet on the rock, and let's hit it. Climb on!

9. **Take in the views:** One of the reasons why I absolutely love climbing is because I'm often climbing in really beautiful areas. **We must get ourselves outside and among beauty.** When you are out there, slow down a bit, look up from your phone, and take in the views, sounds, smells, and the life going on around you. **We are often so busy with**

ourselves that we simply miss the goodness that is around us. We miss the joy, the beauty, the lessons, the smiles, the feel of the chalk and rock in our hands, the warm breeze on our face, the way nervousness settles in our stomach and makes our breathing shallow and quick, the quick thrill of reaching the top and touching the chains, the excitement/anxiety of a new climb, and the awesome views from up top. "Stop and smell the roses," people— but the honest truth is that we don't. We are rushing about like chickens with our heads cut off. We have our eyes and brains constantly ingesting entertainment, and rushing around to pretend that we are busy. Don't! Take in the views and enjoy the ride.

10. **Climb a problem:** Climbers have their own little language. It's kind of fun honestly, and it's one of the things that first led me to use climbing as a form of therapy. For example, when you're bouldering (free-climbing) you don't climb rocks, you climb and solve "a problem." You hold on to "positive holds." You give and receive "beta" from people. You squeeze a hold, and "engage" your feet. You climb deliberately and mind-fully, not mindlessly and desperately. You "spot" others as a way to keep them safe. You ask people who are belaying you to "give you some slack," and when you get a bit nervous and are working through a sketchy piece, you say "watch me close," or "tighten me up." But by far my favorite term is crux. The crux is a specific sequence of moves that is the most difficult part of the climb. The climb gets its rating based on that crux. I just love working through the crux of things. I hope you learn to love it, too.

So, my friend, if you are able and lucky enough to live by climbable rock or a climbing gym, get your climbing on! If you don't, no worries—live as if you were a climber. See you at the rock!

LIFE HACK #26
KEEP A RUNNING LIST OF THINGS
YOU LIKE ABOUT YOURSELF.

Chapter 27
Crocodiles, Oh My!

Hey there, morning glory! I love watching nature shows about the wild and about animals...honestly, it's a bit freaky! I remember when I first watched one of the most dramatic events that happen in nature. Once or twice a year in certain parts of Africa, a huge migration of wildebeests occurs. They travel thousands of miles to greener pastures. This is not an easy migration, and it's often fraught with danger and predators. There is usually not a lot of water, so when the mighty Zambezi river comes into view, the wildebeests rush to drink from it. They are cautious. They've learned to live in a dangerous environment, and yet some of the young inexperienced wildebeests will go all the way into the water to get a drink. What could possibly be wrong with this picture? They're thirsty, here is water, drink it up, right? Wrong! Crocodiles are the problem! Beneath the water are these enormous, prehistoric, Nile crocodiles, weighing over a ton, up to 20 feet long, and with a bite power of 3700 pounds per square inch (PSI). Just to contrast, our bite power is about 200 psi. They have been waiting for the herds to come. They feel the rumble, and wait for the young and ignorant wildebeests to come on down to the water. The crocodiles submerge, and like deadly submarines they attack the unsuspecting wildebeests and drag them away to where the other crocs lie in wait, and tear their victim to shreds.

"Oh my gosh, Iuri, what the heck is your problem! Do you get some sick pleasure out of talking about this gross stuff?" To be honest, I'm kind of fascinated by it. If you've never seen it, look it up on Youtube to see what I'm talking about. Now, you can see where I'm going with this—you're certainly no dumb wildebeest. I've met with people who have gone down to that "water." I've met with those who ignorantly, mindlessly, or defiantly have taken a drink from that poisoned well. In fact, I've met with thousands of them! I've heard their stories and have helped them rise from the ashes and rebuild the wreckage in their lives.

These people are no different from me; they're no different from you. They are looking for what they think they need—for what they think will bring them entertainment, fun, and happiness. They are what I call "magical thinkers." They think they can go down into the water and not get slaughtered like all of the other idiots—they're not like them, they're special (said the dead wildebeest). These people get involved in stealing, cheating, selling and buying drugs, alcohol, pills, pornography, sex, cigarettes…the list is too long to continue— you get the point. They function under some common ideas:

- "I'm only going to do it for a while"
- "I'm just having fun—lighten up, old dude"
- "This helps me" (said the dead wildebeest)
- "There is nothing to do where I live."
- "Everyone is doing it" (sorry, I had to throw that one in there)
- "It's not that bad" (now there is an intelligent philosophy to live your life by)

Anyway, this is sounding more and more like a cautionary tale, and I suppose that it is. Just listen to your old friend Iuri, and stay away from these things. Honestly, don't think and rationalize yourself into doing stuff that is asinine. Use a little bit of intelligence and learn from the history of others. So, next time you suspect that "crocodiles" are under the water, go find a better drinking hole. Later, wildebeest!

LIFE HACK #27
KEEP YOUR LIFE FRESH.
DO SOMETHING DIFFERENT TODAY, AND EVERY DAY AFTER THAT.

Chapter 28
Don't Get Tripped Up

Ready to hit the psychological and emotional gym? Let's go! Not getting tripped up is all about learning how to become more psychologically and emotionally independent, so that your actions are congruent (they match) with your highest ideals, instead of being reactive to what others are doing. Let me give you an example. A young man comes to see me and tells me how much he appreciates his older brother. He loves the way he is treated by him. How he looks out for him. How he takes him to concerts and out to eat. How they play games together, etc. Then he proceeds to tell me how he is always annoyed with his sister. How he sometimes is rude to her. How she is a whiner. How he can't wait to be away from her. I think you see my point a bit here. He's getting tripped up by his sister's behavior. He's not emotionally and psychologically independent, because he is not sticking to what he absolutely knows is the coolest and best thing to do as a brother, which would be for him to treat her awesomely.

Look, we all get tripped up. Part of the reason why we get tripped up is because our brain has a tendency to match what is being offered in front of us. When someone is angry, we have brain-full tendency to get angry back. When someone is petty with us, we have a tendency to be petty back. When someone is rude, our tendency is to return the favor. Notice the psychological and emotional dependence! **What someone else does, thinks, and feels, manages our emotions, instead of us managing our emotions!** I'm telling you this so that you can begin to become more mind-full (deliberate and congruent), and respond in a manner that is awesome and inspiring. This is not always easy to do, but oh man (and woman), It's great to know that you no longer need to be a puppet to someone else's emotions and actions. You can begin to practice this valuable skill by trying the following:

1. Observe when you get sucked into other people's emotions and actions. You can also watch this happen to other people. This will be easy, because we are all doing it my friend, so you will be able to see lots of examples.

2. Stay mind-full by asking yourself these questions: How can I be helpful here? What's the coolest thing I can do right now? How can I invite and promote (remember the 3 questions in Chapter 10) some goodness?

3. When you fall off the wagon (which you will), become overwhelmed by the emotion of a situation, and completely lose your mind, remember to go back and make any necessary reparations so that you can bring yourself back to a mind-full state again.

So, keep your feet beneath you, become aware of other people's emotional temperatures, and learn how to manage your own personal emotional thermostat. I'm proud of you for taking the time to read this—now, let's go and get ripped!

LIFE HACK #28
"EAT A LIVE FROG FIRST THING IN THE MORNING
AND NOTHING WORSE WILL HAPPEN TO YOU THE REST OF THE DAY."
-MARK TWAIN

CHAPTER 29
THOU SHALT JUDGE

Hey friend, I hope life's good. More importantly, I hope you are treating life well. Let's talk about judging and judgment, shall we? I'm assuming that most of you are in some type of schooling experience. If yes, then it's likely that things may seem a bit judgy. You know what I'm talking about—the up-and-down stares, disapproving looks, gossip, and people making wild assumptions (reading a book by its cover). I'm assuming you've noticed this, right? "Dude, Iuri, people should just stop judging, don't you think?" "NO, I don't think that, actually." "What are you talking about, man? I'm sick of people judging me!" "Judging is what people do... It's what you do, and what I'm doing right now." "But even Jesus said not to judge, yo!" "Well, he did say that, but it wasn't the whole of what he said. Let me explain...no, there is too much...let me sum up." So, just for your own knowledge, here are the things that Jesus did say about judgment:

- "Judge not, that ye be not judged. For with what judgment ye judge, ye shall be judged: and with what measure ye mete, it shall be measured unto you again."

- "Condemn not, and ye shall not be condemned: forgive, and ye shall be forgiven: Give, and it shall be given unto you....For with the same measure that ye mete withal it shall be measured to you again."

- "Judge not according to the appearance, but judge righteous judgment."

So let me explain two things to you. First,) **judgment doesn't imply a bad thing. The word judgment is a neutral word**. That means that we can make good and accurate judgments (righteous judgment), and of course we can also judge negatively and inaccurately. So, change that definition inside of your head, and realize that judgment doesn't necessarily mean bad judgment. Second,) we have a brain that is constantly making judgments about our circumstances, people, and things around us, so what do we do? **I think we should judge. In fact, I think we must learn how to judge more accurately and more righteously. I think this is so important that I would place it as part of our purpose in this life**. Once again, look at the passages above: "With what judgment ye judge, ye shall be judged." If you judge others compassionately, understandingly, mercifully, and with love, that same judgment will given to you. That is so brilliant I can hardly stand it!

The problem, of course, is that the brain makes immediate judgments about lots of things. Don't worry, your brain is just being a brain, and doing what it should be doing. **What you must do, then, is use your mind to slow the brain down, gather more information, and make a better judgment.** I hope you picked that up, because that is the formula.

1. **Slow the judgment or withhold the judgment:** When your brain creates immediate judgments, slow it down and realize that the brain is reaching conclusions about situations and people based on previous experiences that don't always translate to the present (remember Chapter 1, and the story of the farmer?).

2. **Gather more information:** This is where you get to work and find out more information about whatever it is that you are looking to make a specific judgment or opinion about.

3. **Make a more accurate and righteous judgment.**

So when you walk into school, or church, or gym class, or the lunch room, or the mall, or wherever you go, and you feel people's eyes on you, and you assume that they may be judging you, you're absolutely right! Their brain is probably making a quick and uneducated judgment about you. Don't get all twisted up inside; their brain is doing exactly what it should be doing—it should be evaluating and assessing their environment. Their judgment might be good; it might be accurate, it might not be. Perhaps their judgment is accurate and helpful; if it is, then I should be thankful for it, and not become offended because I'm being judged (get over yourself). The most important part of this whole argument is learning to mind-fully approach judgment by applying the three steps that I referred to you above. And there it is—you officially have permission to judge! Now go and learn how to do it wisely.

LIFE HACK #29
"NO ONE HAS EVER BECOME POOR BY GIVING."
- ANNE FRANK

Chapter 30
Don't Let Fear Drive Your Life

Greetings, earthling. Ready to talk about fear and anxiety? Let's do it. Fear definitely falls into the category of emotions that I call hard-core. Fear can be very difficult to manage. I often say that fear is a paralytic, meaning that fear can stop or paralyze the body during difficult or scary circumstances. I observe this happening on a daily basis while teaching people to climb, and watch their bodies freeze with fear as they move up the rock wall. **Fear is loud, and it can be completely overwhelming.** I sometimes describe fear as a large and obnoxious giant that walks into the room, knocking chairs and tables over, demanding control. **Now fear isn't all bad of, course, its main function, really, is to warn and protect us from potentially harmful circumstances.** Seen in that light, we can certainly be thankful for it, which I am.

For some, though, fear and anxiety can become rampant and begin to cause problems in their lives. Fear becomes *too* loud. It becomes *too* overwhelming. It begins to take over their life. Fear becomes a conqueror and begins to gobble up psychological and emotional territory inside them. This persistent fear of past, present, and future, is better known as anxiety. **Anxiety is very interesting!** Put on your scientist's coat, grab your clipboard, and let's take a quick look at it. **Anxiety is a disorder of anticipation. This means that your brain can project itself into the future, and imagine a scary "what if" scenario with such force, and clarity, that your body will begin to experience anxiety, even though nothing is really happening.** Isn't that amazing? Let me give you an example: Someone who fears flying doesn't have to be in an airplane to experience the full force of anxiety; they just need to imagine being in a closed airplane at 30,000 feet. Another example is someone who struggles going to school because they are anxious. They don't only experience fear or anxiety at school; it begins as soon as they wake up, and their brain begins to project (like a movie) how bad the day is going to be. The result? They feel sick to their stomach, they don't feel well, they're a bit keyed-up, and they finally decide not to go. Which brings me to our next factoid about fear: **anxiety is a disorder of avoidance; in fact, this is one of its central features. This simply means that fear pushes us to avoid the things that cause us anxiety.** The problem occurs, of course, when fear causes us to avoid good, meaningful, and important things like school, work, church, being with friends, speaking to people, helping others, exercising, eating, sleeping, asking someone out, being proactive or taking initiative, and admitting to mistakes. This is when fear becomes too much and begins to drive one's life. **We cannot allow fear to take over our lives, because when it does, our lives become very small indeed.** I want you to make a commitment to yourself right now. Repeat after me: **"I must not fear. Fear is the mind-killer. Fear is the little-death that brings total obliteration. Without fear, I will die only once. I will face my fear. I will permit it to pass over me and through me. And when it has gone past I will turn the inner eye to see its path. Where the fear has gone there will be nothing. Only I will remain."** If you struggle with anxiety, I want you to remember this, memorize it even. Some warriors in the past would recite this litany (prayer or invocation), to overcome their feelings of fear.

I like this saying, I think it's inspiring, but I don't want you to *fear* fear. I don't want you to fear its arrival, or how it feels inside you, because this only grows your anxiety. Does that make sense? **Fear of fear increases fear.** Often people's anxiety becomes so high that they begin to experience panic attacks. Panic attacks are not pleasant at all. They happen when the body's fight, flight, and freeze mechanism sends the message that something terrible is about to happen, so the body releases massive amounts of adrenaline and other chemicals into the brain, to the point that our hearts speed up, we experience nausea, we become extremely restless (even shaky), and our brains begin to think very rapidly and out of control. Panic attacks are so painful that people will often check themselves into the emergency room because they think they are going to die. It's very intense. It is at this point that people who have anxiety begin to fear anxiety and panic even more. This, of course, creates more anxiety for them. I often tell people, **the moment you stop fearing your panic attacks is the moment you stop having them.** It's not easy to do, but it's definitely a worthwhile goal.

Let's get back to not fearing fear. What we must do instead is understand it. As we listen to the message of fear (you better prepare and get ready), we begin to have a different relationship with it. The brain is really not trying to harm us; in fact, it is attempting to protect us. For those who struggle with anxiety disorder, their brains becomes obsessed and stuck on things that could go wrong. As the brain becomes overwhelmed, it begins to sound the alarm, and they experience it in their bodies as anxiety. Perhaps this short quote will help you to refocus your brain and realize that "nothing in this life is to be feared. It is to be understood. Now is the time to understand, so that we can fear less." This quote resonates with me; does it with you? That is why you are reading this specific chapter. **Learning and understanding the anatomy of fear protects you from experiencing high levels of anxiety and panic in the future. We are no longer running from and refusing to look at it. We are now willing to look at, study, talk about, and work with the dang thing!**

If you are experiencing high levels of fear and anxiety, perhaps it's time for you to talk to someone about it. You don't need to wear it like a badge ("Hey everyone, check it out— I have anxiety!"), but perhaps it's time for you to talk to a parent, school counselor, or religious leader, who can point you in the right direction. **Remember, talking is powerful and can help provide you with some needed relief, and the path toward meaningful solutions.** Don't hold it in. It doesn't have to be a secret (secrets kill us...seriously). Be mind-full here, not brain-full, and talk to someone who cares and who can help.

We can't let fear and anxiety become a bully in our lives. We can't let it become a thief and rob us of living a full and joyful life. We cannot just stand by while it runs us

into the ground. It's time to get serious about our psychology and our emotional well-being, and begin to seek for help and solutions. I don't care how long it takes, begin now! Love ya!

LIFE HACK #30
PARK YOUR CAR FAR AWAY AND WALK SLOWLY.

CHAPTER 31
APOLOGIZE AND FORGIVE

There are many things in this life that are worth learning about and that will improve the quality of your relationships. One of those is your ability to apologize for your mistakes, and to learn to forgive. There is a wonderful courage and humility in people who willingly accept their faults and have the mind-full ability to apologize and attempt to make reparations for the mistakes they've made. **The foolish and brain-full man is proud, and afraid to admit his faults. I'm telling you, this cannot be you! If you have a hard time apologizing and making repairs, it's time to up your game and move toward a more enlightened and intelligent way of being.** Readily and quickly apologize for any hurt you cause to others. Don't carry that burden around your neck—get rid of it.

Remember that your behavior is a symptom of your psychology and ideology. In other words, the things you believe about yourself, others, and the world around you ultimately show up in your behavior. So if apologizing (behavior) is difficult for you, that means that you are in possession of some internal ideas (psychology) that make it hard to apologize. Let me share what some of these behaviors and ideas could be:

- **You are keeping score:** You don't apologize because you feel that others have wronged you more than you have hurt them.

- **You become angry:** Have you ever become angry after you have hurt someone? Do you wonder why? It is because you are proud and afraid to humble yourself enough to admit and apologize for a fault. It is because you have betrayed yourself, and now you must repair it. This requires that you drop your own pride and conceit, and accept that you have hurt someone.

- **You blame other people:** You hide your mistakes by blaming other people for them. It's a little switcheroo! It's interesting, isn't it? You've treated someone else unjustly, rudely, unkindly, yet you blame them. It's a clear sign that you're walking around with blinders on. No worries, it's time to remove the blinders and see and think clearly. Don't blame others for your personal mistakes; readily accept responsibility for them.

- **You justify your behavior:** Instead of apologizing, you justify what you did because of something that was done to you. "Well, if Susan hadn't been such a jerk, I wouldn't have hit her over the head with the frying pan!" Here are some other examples: "Everybody cheats," "He started it," "Well, did you see what he/she did to me?" Don't justify or make excuses for your wrongdoing—accept it, apologize, and move on.

- **You become the martyr:** Here is what this sounds like: "I know, I know, I never do anything right," "I'm so stupid," or "I'm such a loser and a failure." Instead of owning your junk and apologizing, you instead slip into a pity party about how everyone hates you, and how big a failure you are. Take the easier and wiser path, and just apologize, for heaven's sake.

- **You are stuck in the "life is not fair" (the F-word) mentality:** I'm telling you, the mindset of fairness is poison to the mind. It turns and twists you against others and the world around you. When you are stuck in this place, you don't see or admit to blame within you, because it's all outside of you. It's everyone else's fault! It's time to pack up and move out of this inferior mind-scape.

I'm telling you these things so that you will **walk through this life with your eyes wide open, with a clear understanding that you are riddled with holes and imperfections, aware that you will fail often and greatly and, perhaps more**

importantly, humble and meek enough to admit your mistakes, indiscretions, and faults to others. It's so refreshing and attractive to meet people who personify humility. Their hearts are open. Their minds are alert and at ease with themselves and the world. Their behavior toward the world is gentle, and their walk with their friends is a peaceful one. They are giants of people. It's time for you to become a giant as well.

That brings us to forgiveness. If there ever is a need for something in this world, it is for forgiveness. In our families, our schools, and with our friends. Our ability to forgive or not forgive says something about ourselves and our relationship to the world, as well as the quality of our interactions with others around us. **I believe that forgiveness is a natural occurrence when our minds and hearts are clear and in line with the truth.** Will you read what I am about to teach you about forgiveness, so that you can learn this divine art? Perhaps we should define what forgiveness is and what it is not.

- **Forgiveness is not forgetting:** The old adage, "Forgive and forget," is just plain wrong, and a wholly inaccurate expectation that only creates further frustration and resentment. The truth is our brain cannot forget. It retains those memories for us in an effort to protect us from future harm. In addition, our brains are best at recalling intense moments and memories.

- **Forgiveness is not condoning:** When we forgive we are not condoning any form of abuse; instead, we are promoting redemption, hope, and beauty. Forgiveness is our gift to the world.

- **Forgiveness is not immediately trusting:** I can imagine a variety of scenarios in which my forgiveness of an event or individual is completely separate from the degree of trust that I may place on the individual or circumstance in the future. That trust may grow over time, yet I feel perfectly at peace in placing some measure of protection to try to stop the event from happening again. **Forgiveness is perfectly logical, not illogical.**

- **Forgiveness can include a complete emotional healing, but it doesn't necessarily have to:** People will often ask me, "Iuri, I feel that I have forgiven, but sometimes I still feel afraid and have thoughts of anger and bitterness." I don't believe that forgiveness has to include a guarantee that releases us from the cross that we sometimes may have to shoulder. This is one of the great realities of life—namely, that we will have to carry the consequences of others' faults and sins upon our backs. Resisting that truth will cause you to live in bitterness and resentment. Accepting it, on the other hand, will liberate you and allow you to experience a calmer and more peaceful existence.

- **Forgiveness is not ignoring what occurred:** In fact, an important part of healing properly involves communicating about it with someone who has proven worthy of your trust. I often remind clients that **when we are able to talk about something, our ability to control that something increases.** When we can't or won't talk about something, that something gains control over us. Recognize that a conversation may have to occur repeatedly and across a span of time. It's not about dragging something out of the closet and beating it to death; it's about decreasing any level of shame, guilt, or hurt that is still residing within our memory.

- **Forgiveness is not a return to things as they were:** People often express a desire for things to go back to how they once were. Sameness is not what we are after. Trauma changes us. So a return to something old is not only unrealistic but potentially problematic, as one's expectations of what should be happening don't match up with what is happening in the present.

- **Forgiveness is not dependent on others' behaviors:** Forgiveness is a psychologically, emotionally, and spiritually mature practice. Whether you have a spiritual foundation or not, the revolutionary words of Jesus are consistent with this enlightened understanding of ourselves and others: *"Ye have heard that it hath been said, Thou shalt love thy neighbor,*

and hate thine enemy. But I say unto you, love your
enemies, bless them that curse you, do good to them that
hate you, and pray for them which despitefully use you, and
persecute you;...for he maketh his sun to rise on the evil and
on the good, and sendeth rain on the just and on the unjust."
For both secular and religious individuals, this is a hard and
yet powerful doctrine. What would we have to understand to
be able to act in such a way? What is it that we would have to
realize about ourselves or others to respond from such a
place of love and peace?

So, what is forgiveness? Fred Luskin, a teacher in the art of
forgiveness and author of *Forgive for Good*, states that forgiveness
consists of two parts: (1) making peace; and (2) achieving that peace
by resolving our objection to life, our objection to what has
happened to us, and the fact that it wasn't what we wanted to have
happened. **Forgiveness can be defined as letting go of hate,
resentment, bitterness, or ill will toward another human
being (this includes us).** The practice of forgiveness has been
shown to reduce anger, hurt, depression, and stress, and to lead to
greater feelings of hope, peace, compassion and self-confidence.
Practicing forgiveness leads to healthy relationships as well as better
physical health. It also influences our attitude and opens the heart to
kindness, beauty, and love. Mr. Luskin also suggests that at the heart
of forgiveness is gratitude and compassion. **In a way, the
individual who inhabits this philosophy of gratitude and
compassion, is the individual who is able to make peace
and be fully accepting of what has occured in the past.
When we accept what has happened (it has right?), then we
can move forward, instead of staying myred and stuck on
how unfair, unjust, and victimized we have been. When we
give up resisting, then we can finally get to work.** My hope is
that you will shift from the retarding mindset of "What can I expect
from this world?" to "What does this world expect from me?" As you
begin to make these transformations over time, you will begin to
shift from powerless to powerful. From victim to teacher. From hurt
to courageous. From fearful to loving! I'm surely not attempting to
sound preachy here. I have no concept of your pain, nor do I have

any idea of the horror that some of you have been subjected to. **But let me suggest, from my place of accepted ignorance, that there is peace and hope. That there is liberation and growth, and that it is possible!**

The world yearns for redemption! **Redemption is the hope that despite our stupidity, immaturity, ignorance, wrongdoing, selfishness, abuse, and neglect, we can return, redeemed and transformed, and grow toward a brighter existence.**

_____What would we have to understand or realize to be forgiving of others and ourselves? I'm reminded of Marianne Williamson's words: *"The choice to follow love through to its completion is the choice to seek completion within ourselves. The point at which we shut down on others is the point at which we shut down on life. We heal as we heal others, and we heal others by extending our perceptions past their weaknesses. Until we have seen someone's darkness, we don't really know who that person is. Until we have forgiven someone's darkness, we don't really know what love is. Forgiving others is the only way to forgive ourselves, and forgiveness is our greatest need."* My hope is for forgiveness to become a natural practice for you. Something that is not forced, which flows from you simply because you see yourself and others in a clearer light. As I have studied and observed those who are forgiving, I find that they possess one or more of three specific ideologies:

- **They practice radical acceptance: When the dream we hoped for dies in favor of reality, we must act from within that reality, and not from where we think we should be.** Fred Luskin explains that resentment and bitterness are our own creation when we refuse to act from a place "that is," and instead react from "where we think things ought to be." The perceived gap between what has happened and what we wish would have happened, is what Dan Milman describes as the genesis of our suffering. He says that "stress and anxiety happen when we resist what is." Life is not a restaurant, where we get to show our ignorant indignation when something we want from the menu is not available. That sense of entitlement and "I deserve" psychology is complete nonsense! It will not yield a positive outcome. It will instead promote an obsessive hunger and thirst that will never be filled. This willingness— this submissive acceptance—assumes a deeper spiritual truth, a purpose that is inherent in things: **the realization that life and people don't give us what we want, but what we need to grow and evolve.** C.S. Lewis expresses this idea when he describes us as rudimentary blocks of granite, with God as the sculptor. The painful blows of chisel and hammer leave us hurt, overwhelmed, and fearful, yet those same blows shape us and lead us to be partakers of the Divine nature.

- **They realize that we are all beggars in need of mercy, understanding, and kindness:** Those for whom forgiveness is a natural endeavor have a true understanding of their own faults, misgivings, and potential for serious error. Jesus once again challenged the perceptions of the day by relating this simple parable: "*Two men went up into the temple to pray; the one a Pharisee, and the other a publican. The Pharisee stood and prayed thus with himself, God, I thank thee, that I am not as other men are, extortioners, unjust, adulterers, or even as this publican. I fast twice in the week, I give tithes of all that I possess. And the publican, standing afar off, would not lift up so much as his eyes unto heaven, but smote upon his breast, saying, God be merciful to me a sinner. I tell you, this man went down to his house justified rather than the other: for every one that exalteth himself shall be abased; and he that humbleth himself shall be exalted.*" Yet another time, He revealed the primitive tendency we have to obsess about other's faults while disregarding our own, when He asked, "*How canst thou say to thy brother, Brother, let me pull out the mote that is in thine eye, when thou thyself beholdest not the beam that is in thine own eye? Thou hypocrite, cast out first the beam out of thine own eye, and then shalt thou see clearly to pull out the mote that is in thy brother's eye.*" **We** must come to the realization that we are all traveling through this life together, learning to love and learning to be loved, learning to forgive others as well as ourselves. Forgiveness is logical! It makes sense! Forgiveness is the natural manifestation of an enlightened understanding.

- **We are mere mortals:** Dieter F. Uchtdorf's declaration that "**we mortals are scarcely more than awkward, faltering toddlers**" helps us to view ourselves and others from a more accurate and compassionate perspective. I find it interesting that as the light of my knowledge and experience expands, so does the realization of my ignorance. **Accepting our ignorance not as a curse, but as something that we are called to attend to, and bring the light of truth into, is one of the primary purposes of our existence.** This powerful form of meekness and humility will fill you with gratitude and an effortless compassion toward others. The critical realization is that much of who we are was not consciously and mind-fully chosen by us. That the people, culture, and the environment around which we were raised have dramatically impacted our way of being. **It's difficult to admit that I too could perpetrate horror upon others, yet, had I been raised differently, had I been exposed to the horror, abuse, brainwashing, and terrible circumstances that others have been, I too might be wandering through this life causing pain in the same manner that pain is inflicted upon me.** And yet every individual has moments where the divine light shines through. These "Eureka" moments are calls to arise and seek help, to examine our lives and discover the tragic ideals that rest within us, wreaking havoc individually and interpersonally. **Forgiveness of ourselves and others is not only the honor and responsibility to influence the lives of others, but the permission to try again.**

Finally, how do you begin this process of forgiving? It's helpful to have a plan, a structure that can help you to move from where you are to the peace that awaits just beyond. Here are a few steps for you to consider as you commit to being forgiving:

1. **Allow yourself space:** Remember who you are. It's okay to feel honestly. Give yourself permission to be human. We can get so very hurt, and life can get incredibly difficult at times. Remember that forgiveness may not necessarily create complete emotional relief. There may be pain, trauma, and regret still associated with whatever event or act occurred. Our purpose is to reduce the impact of these emotions so that we can act out our lives in ways that are meaningful and purposeful to us, instead of being acted upon by the emotional events of our past.

2. **Remember to be mind-full:** As you become more full of mind, you will recognize the trauma and hurt that is stored in the brain, and realize that it is not a representation of the future. Recognize the fear, pain, paranoia, trauma, and insecurity as tools that the brain has used to protect you from more pain. You are older now, more experienced. It is time to upgrade your current operating system. Time to evolve beyond what your brain is presenting. Forgiveness is a process and a mindset. Something that is engaged in purposefully and patiently. Slowly by slowly, line upon line, this new philosophy will become the norm, and your whole body will cooperate as your internal philosophies and behaviors join forces congruently.

3. **Acknowledge what has happened and identify how you feel about it:** Events and circumstances can be so brutal at times that we may become lost and overwhelmed. During such moments we may lose consciousness and not fully understand where we really are or what we should do. Take time to identify how you feel about things by: (1) journaling or writing about the event; (2) processing those events with a close friend, a family member, a magnificent

clinician, or a religious leader whom you trust; and (3) making a deliberate effort toward forgiveness.

4. **Generate a plan:** Remember that forgiveness is about you finding peace, blaming less, and taking meaningful and purposeful action. Try these steps as you engage and invest in the process of forgiveness:

   a. Make a commitment to yourself that you will engage in this process and will do whatever it takes to feel better.

   b. Engage and invest in the process by picking a good book that will promote positive insight.

   c. Ask yourself, "What would I have to realize about myself to forgive?"

   d. Ask yourself, "What would I like to feel instead of the pain and anger I am feeling now?"

   e. Ask yourself, "What would have to happen for me to make peace with what has occurred?"

   f. Dr. Hallowell, author of *Dare to Forgive*, suggests that we look for the "hook." "The hook is what is holding you back—it' the portion of the misdeed that is causing you to hold on to your anger and resentment."

   g. Lastly, take courage and ask this daring question: I can be grateful for [fill in with whatever event or circumstance] because [fill in with an appropriate reason]? Be brave. Ponder, pray, meditate deeply upon this last question. Open your heart for another potential outcome.

I know that this chapter has been significantly longer than the rest. It is meant to be a tool for you. Perhaps something that you can return to for some guidance in the future. Learn it, use it, believe it. Remember that forgiveness is natural—don't resist it. Forgiveness is the manifestation of an internal philosophy that either supports it or rejects it. I wish you the very best.

Life Hack #31
"What I am looking for is not out there, it is in me."
-Helen Keller

Chapter 32
Do Good and Let it Be

Hey soldier, I'm convinced today is going to be an excellent day! To make it particularly great, you must **learn to be a giver and a creator, not a taker in this life.** I'm reminded of a short little story that I love.

A senior and a junior monk were traveling together when they came upon a very rich woman who was being carried in a chair by her four servants. The rains had fallen, it was muddy, and the river was full and quick. They sought to cross the river but had a difficult time doing so because the woman had brought along many gifts. The servants were fumbling about and she was in her usual foul mood. Upon watching the scene for a few moments, the senior monk approached the woman, placed her on his back, crossed the river, and let her down on the other side. When he joined the junior monk, they traveled together in silence for many hours, until they arrived at their temple. As they approached the temple doors, the junior disciple finally spoke: "Master, today you touched a woman [they're not supposed to] that was rude and selfish to others, you carried her across the river, and she didn't even thank you or anyone else." The master, in his wisdom, responded, "Fellow brother, I set her down on the other side of the river. Why are you still carrying her?"

I enjoy this simple story simply because it illustrates the point that **when you give something, or give of yourself to others, you would be wise to remove any expectation of return. Learn to give because it is wise and good to give. Give your friendship, your kindness, the very best of you, and then simply let it be.** Jesus said it beautifully, **"Let not thy left hand know what thy right hand doeth."** Isn't that brilliant? Instead of giving with your left while having your right hand held out, waiting to receive (what's in it for me, or, what are you going to do for me now?), give freely and without expectation. How do you do this? You have to own the things you do, and why you do them. **You must give because you believe that it is better to give. You are kind because as an enlightened person you realize that kindness breeds kindness, and because it works better. You forgive because you believe in forgiveness. You seek learning and growth in life because ignorance is not bliss, it's a jail, and you want to be a free person who is incredibly joyous.** See what I'm saying? You do what you do because you believe in those things, not because others want you to do them, or because you think you're going to get a little sticker or pat on the back.

Let me also say that no personal characteristic is more unattractive than entitlement, or an attitude of "I deserve this." You may know some takers in your circles. These are individuals who, for whatever reason, believe they are entitled to things (phones, cars, computers, fancy clothes, gifts, toys, etc.). In their heads, they believe people should treat them a certain way. They believe they deserve (uh-oh, the D-word) to have things, and that they should be given them simply because they want them, or because Johnny or Mary down the street have them. Do not be this individual. Make a commitment today to **be a giver and a creator, and not a taker. No one owes you anything! What people in their goodness give you or offer to you, be immensely grateful for. If there are things you want and desire, set your mind on them and go create an intelligent way to get them.**

My friend, it is joy, excitement, fun, and evolution that I hope for you. More importantly, you must seek it as well, and on that road of discovery you will find that you must give without the poison of expectation. I'm out (mic drop...thud).

LIFE HACK #32
IF YOU WANT IT, GIVE IT.

CHAPTER 33
WHAT ARE YOU AIMING AT?

What you are aiming at, determines what you see. Huh? Yes, my daughters have a little quote hanging on their wall, "What you seek is seeking you." The concept isn't meant to be mysterious—it has everything to do with the simple and true concept that we always find the things we are seeking. If you are looking for faults, you will find them. If you are looking to blame, you will find many reasons to do so. If you are looking for how unfair (F-bomb—refer to Chapter 6) life is, or your parents are, or people at school are...ta-da! You will find it. Conversely, **if you are aiming your powerful consciousness at beauty, I guarantee you will discover it. If you seek for gratitude, you will always find it. If you look for the goodness in others, you will uncover it.** One of the most common phrases uttered by the Master Teacher Himself (Christ) is exactly that: "Ask, and it shall be given you; seek, and ye shall find; knock, and it shall be opened unto you." As a result of this truism, two questions are of significant importance to you:

1. **What are you seeing out there?** Because if you are seeing it, that means it is what you are looking for. Isn't that interesting? I'm telling you, your psychology and perception is everything.

2. **What are you aiming at?** Now is the time for you to mind-fully aim your instrument (brain) deliberately, instead of haphazardly and randomly.

This goes back to one of our brain's most interesting thinking errors—confirmation bias (Chapter 17). If you recall, **your brain will naturally seek to confirm the things you already believe.** So, when you walk into school today, and your overall belief about the people in your school is that they are snobby, or that they are cliquey, or that they are stupid, selfish, fake, uncaring, or rude, guess what your brain will discover for you? "BOOM!" Yes, that is the sound of your mind being blown.

Don't worry, this is not a permanent condition of your brain—it is something that we can manipulate and transform. **Your brain is much like a telescope or a microscope—the more you aim at those things that foster and nurture happiness, goodness, and peace, the more you will discover them.** Don't look for things that promote jealousy, bitterness, and anger. If you are constantly feeling those things, that is a good sign that your mental telescope is aimed there...shift it.

I'm not asking you to ignore things. I'm not asking you to be fake. I understand that there is tragedy and scandal out there. I know that we are ignorant and, as a result, we are often rude, uncaring, egocentric, and ungrateful. We must address those things, but let's do it from a place of power and solutions, not poor judgment and condemnation. **So from now on, aim at solutions, not blame; aim at what you can do, not at what you can't do; aim at gratitude, not at what you don't have; aim at being friendly, not at how crappy people are being to you; aim at hope, because hope is real.** Bye-bye.

Life Hack #33
Hang out the "Welcome" sign.

Chapter 34
Become a Hotspot

You're no dummy—I'm sure you know what a hotspot is, but just in case you don't, here goes. A hotspot is when you use a device, connected to cellular data to act as a source of wifi for another tablet, computer, or mobile device that does not have cellular data or internet access. The technology is brilliant, but before I completely geek out on you, let me help you **become a hotspot—a source of awesomeness, safety, and friendship—for others.**

I've always enjoyed the simple but true adage, **"A rising tide lifts all boats."** Simply stated, the goodness of one raises the goodness in others. Marianne Williamson, in her classic work *A Return to Love*, writes:

"Our deepest fear is not that we are inadequate. Our deepest fear is that we are powerful beyond measure. It is our light, not our darkness, that most frightens us. We ask ourselves, Who am I to be brilliant, gorgeous, talented, and fabulous? Actually, who are you not to be? You are a child of God. ***Your playing small does not serve the world. There is nothing enlightened about shrinking so that other people will not feel insecure around you.*** *We are all meant to shine, as children do. We were born to make manifest the glory of God that is within us. It is not just in some of us; it is in everyone and* ***as we let our own light shine, we unconsciously give others permission to do the same. As we are liberated from our own fear, our presence automatically liberates others."***

There are many excellent parts to this small poem that are worth of mentioning and studying, but the part we will utilize today is right at the end, when she says that "as we let our own light shine, we unconsciously give others permission to do the same. As we are liberated from our own fear, our presence automatically liberates others." Is this true? **Are we really that contagious? Does what we believe, what we do, and who we are really impact the world around us?** There is no question that this is accurate, especially to those that are in closest proximity to you. **Imagine that your kindness actually inspires kindness from others; your laughter incites others to laugh; your courage motivates courage in others; your strength sparks strength in others; your willingness to forgive emboldens other to forgive, as well; as you love the ones around you, they too are more likely to love.** I want you to **spread your smile like a wildfire!** I want you to be a hotspot for everything that is good in this world.

I remember a comedian whose whole act was about the idea that stupid people should wear signs around their necks stating, "I'm stupid," so that others would know what to expect when they would be around them. It's very funny—you should look it up (Bill Engvall). I want you to wear a different kind of sign around your neck. **I want you to throw out the welcome sign to others.** I don't know what sign you've got hanging around your neck ("Don't screw with me"; "I'm too cool for you"; "I'm a pushover"; "I'm not smart"; "I don't care about anything"; "I'm scared and you should be too"), but it's time for you to bring out the sign that says "Welcome!" Here are some other signs that are worth considering:

- "You've got a friend in me"
- "I'm loyal"
- "I try to make good choices"
- "I'm kind"
- "I'm a safe harbor"
- "Judgment-free zone"
- "I don't gossip"
- "I'm fun"
- "No drama llama"
- "Happiness here"

- "I'm not afraid"

- "I'm approachable"

- "I'm a disciple of Christ

- We're the same, you and I

- Rise and Shine

- Hey good lookin' what you got cookin'?

What sign do you have hanging around your neck? If you asked your mom or dad, or your siblings, or your friends, what would they tell you? Perhaps more importantly, what sign do you want to hang around your neck? Think this over, pick the wisest and then hang it out. Now go and become a hotspot for awesomeness.

LIFE HACK #34
IF SOMEONE OFFERS YOU A MINT, TAKE IT!

CHAPTER 35
THE ART OF GRATITUDE

Aahh...the amazing sound of quiet. I love a good, still morning when I can put my thoughts together, meditate, and pray. The practice of meditation and prayer are immensely healthy, in part because they focus on being thank-full. There is an absolute correlation between gratitude and joy—**the more grateful we find ourselves, the more peace and joy we will experience.** Gratitude is a mindset. It is a way of looking at the world and interpreting it.

I'm reminded of the small story in the bible when Jesus passes by ten individuals afflicted with leprosy. They plead with Christ to heal them. Jesus tells them to go and show themselves to the priests. The lepers obey him, and as they're going on their way something miraculous happens—they become healed. Of the ten lepers that were afflicted by this terminal, flesh-eating disease, only one returns to Jesus and falls at his feet, thanking him. Jesus asks him, "Were there not ten cleansed? But where are the nine?" But the other nine were nowhere to be found.

In this life, and particularly in relationships, we must be that one, not the other nine! Oh, this small story carries such a punch, such a critical and simple message. **Gratitude is as much a gift to the receiver as it is to the giver.** Gratitude is a game-changer. It is attractive. It is the sign of a clear and healthy mind. It is the fruit of a humble perspective that recognizes that so much of what we have is gifted to us, with no effort of our own.

I find that people who are grateful possess a set of powerful and transcendent beliefs that allow them to see and experience life in a remarkable way. Here are some of those beliefs and practices:

- **They believe that life is happening for them, not to them:** There is a purpose to life, and all moments prepare us for the very next moment.

- **They believe in growth, expansion, and evolution:** Remember that all moments can give us experience and ultimately be for our good. I know that in certain circumstances that can be a hard pill to swallow, but it's true...so true! I beg you to adopt that mindset.

- **They practice gratitude:** Whether through prayer, meditation, or a gratitude journal, these wise people realize that, as with all things, we must practice and learn the language of gratitude. Want to feel happier? Answer these questions at the end of each day. What 3 things am I grateful for today? And why? Train your eyes and your brain to seek for things you are grateful for.

- **They are humble:** They do not see themselves as people who are owed things, or entitled, or even deserving (the D-word). They marvel at the good that is in their lives. They notice the small things, the medium things, and the large things, and they are grateful for them. They are willing, teachable, and open to what life has to teach them. Their heart is soft; thus, they will be happy.

Thank-fullness is a sign of being mind-full. Remember that the brain is a survival organ. It is constantly looking for ways to keep us safe from the harmful things in our environment. As such, it often looks for what has gone wrong and what could go wrong in the future. The brain is often critical and prone to fault-finding. We cannot allow these brain-full tendencies to take over our psychology. The cure is mind-full gratitude. **Gratitude is the art of good-finding, and discovering meaning and goodness from our earthly travels.** Practice it, seek for it, and find it in your daily life from the moment you wake to the moment you sleep. Happy practicing!

Life Hack #35

Want to calm your brain? Learn to calm the body.
Learn how to progressively relax the muscles in your body.

CHAPTER 36
ASK BETTER QUESTIONS

Words are so powerful and meaningful, especially the words we repetitively tell ourselves. Like a spell, our words, phrases, and questions carry within them a prophetic influence on our identity and our mental health. It's obvious that I'm a fan of questions and the potential they have to discover and create meaningful and long-term change. **Questions tell our brain what to focus on, what to think about, and what to block out. The questions we ask ourselves can either move us toward liberation and revelation or toward imprisonment and distortion.**

When anxious individuals and those afflicted by depressive thoughts and emotions walk into my office, I honestly feel excited. There is so much I want to tell them—so many things to discover about themselves that can immediately begin to transform and diminish the impact of those thoughts and feelings. Depressed and anxious individuals often have very oppressive thinking habits, as well as a dysfunctional relationship with their emotions. In addition, they ask themselves terrible questions. Questions that contribute to and maintain the anxious and depressive cycles they find themselves in. They ask, "Why does this only happen to me?" or "What if...[fill in any negative scenario]?" or, "Will this ever end, and what if it doesn't?" Here is one that I heard recently in my office: "If he's lying about this, what else is he going to lie about?" Remember that these questions are like commands to the brain. In essence, we are telling the brain, "Brain, focus on this! Search this out; be on the lookout for when this happens again, and when it does, bring it to my attention." These questions will either exacerbate your current state of suffering and fear, or launch you into one. **Remember that when the brain focuses on and visualizes intensely about the past or the future, the body is going to feel it. This is**

called the brain-body connection. Like a dream. In a dream something is only occurring in the brain, and yet the body is experiencing it as if it is actually happening. Well, it doesn't just happen when you are asleep, it happens when you are fully awake and focused. These negative questions create a negative trance, or a highly focused state. As the brain runs all of the negative scenarios and answers all of the negative-leaning questions, it releases chemicals that increase anxiety and stress, and the body experiences the effects of those chemicals. In anxiety, there is an acceleration, as the brain and body become agitated and brace for certain impact (pain, fear, harm, betrayal, failure). In depression, the brain is playing a hopeless and helpless tale, a very real one at that. As chemicals are released, the body begins to sink into a state of resignation, pain, and hopelessness. In an effort to protect itself and its host, the brain begins to create a barrier between ourselves and the scary, painful world. As a result, the body feels numb. Not only does it block the intensity of the negativity, but it also blocks those things that once brought you joy or pleasure.

There are deeper things at work here, but it's important for you to see how questions can get things started, and will surely maintain them. **Revolutions start with questions.** So which questions can you ask that will incite an internal revolution to freedom and confidence? Ask one of these questions, or a variation of it, to get your brain kick-started in the right direction:

- **What can I do right now that would be helpful?** It's simple and effective. Notice the message you are sending to the brain. "Hey Brain, can you search for some options that can assist me?" If the brain is already drifting toward helplessness and hopelessness, you may have to persist and ask again. Write it down! Begin small. Anything that will get the engine turning; anything that will spark a little flame. Even if it doesn't, anything that falls within the meaningful, positive, building, or expanding range is hopeful and will ultimately yield a positive fruit. **Sometimes we have to keep on living until we feel like living.** Many times anxiety and stress can build because we are neglecting things. Take some form of small, medium, or large action

~~that will address~~ what needs to be done, or whatever you have procrastinated. If no ~~resolution can be reached,~~ start anew, and commit to doing something different from this moment forward, and begin it right now.

- **What does life expect from me this very moment?** Viktor Frankl captured this idea in his life-changing book *Man's Search for Meaning*. Viktor and others were prisoners in a German concentration camp and afflicted by the most extreme of circumstances. Of those prisoners, he said, *"**It did not really matter what we expected from life, but rather what life expected from us.** We needed to stop asking about the meaning of life, and instead to think of ourselves as those who were being questioned by life—daily and hourly. Our answer must consist, not in talk and meditation, but in right action and in right conduct. Life ultimately means taking the responsibility to find the right answer to its problems and to fulfill the tasks which it constantly sets for each individual."* This is a challenging thought, especially when we feel victimized and unjustly dealt with, yet a great truth is manifested in these words. **Each one of us is part of this great equation called life. Like variables, when our value changes, the outcome changes. Stretch your mind beyond where it is stuck. Peer just beyond the great wall that stands between where you are and where you want to be. Don't be afraid to do what you don't feel like doing. Don't feel fake for trying! Your truth is not in inaction; it is in action. It is not in being stuck and feeling helpless; it is in creating and expanding. It is not in pity, but in courage.**

Notice how these questions direct the brain to consider what can be done by you, instead of how helpless you are to the circumstances around you. Try it out! Next time you catch your brain veering toward a depressive or anxious cliff, it may be because you are engaging your brain in a negative way and filling it with negative questions. Stop that process by asking these simple, proactive questions, and then take action. In sum, ask better questions, and get better answers.

Life Hack #36
Don't say "ain't" 'cause your mother will faint and your father will die, and I will call the FBI.

Chapter 37
Every Moment Prepares You for the Very Next Moment

I remember listening to a story about Nelson Mandela. I assume you know who he is, but if you don't, it is worthwhile finding out more. He's a fascinating person. In a nutshell, Nelson Mandela was a South African anti-apartheid revolutionary. Initially, he supported a non-violent approach to opposing British rule and abolishing apartheid (a system of segregation based on race), though he later supported groups who proactively attempted to sabotage the current government. He was imprisoned for treason, and in 1962 was sentenced to life in prison. He served for 27 years, at which point he was released, re-engaged in his previous quest to end apartheid, and became South Africa's first black president. Mandela was later interviewed by a man who asks him how he survived under the injustice of his long imprisonment. Mandela responded by saying he didn't "survive"; he *prepared*. This is a magnificent philosophy, one which, if adopted, can become life-changing for you. **The ability to see that each moment of our lives is the preparation for the next!** To recognize that this life is a vehicle for us to evolve, to grow and expand! This philosophy, perhaps more than any other, teaches us that **within each experience are the seeds of potential growth, of increased vision, experience, and a richer existence.**

Joseph Smith, the American prophet, told of an experience wherein he was falsely imprisoned and made to suffer greatly. While imprisoned in a most severe environment, there were great injustices that were being done to the Mormon people, and Joseph's profound sadness and discouragement were nearly more than he could endure. He reported praying to God and receiving these few verses of magnificent revelation wherein God stated, *"And if thou shouldst be cast into the pit, or into the hands of murderers, and the sentence of death passed upon thee; if thou be cast into the deep; if the billowing surge conspire against thee; if fierce winds become thine enemy; if the heavens gather blackness, and all the elements combine to hedge up the way; and above all, if the very jaws of hell shall gape open the mouth wide after thee, know thou, my son, that all these things shall give thee experience, and shall be for thy good."* **This is a powerful doctrine that, if instilled within the walls of our hearts, will liberate us to find personal meaning in our moments of greatest sadness, tragedy, loss, and disappointment. It invites us to step beyond the great injustices and tragedies of this life, with the recognition that as we carry the burdens and vicissitudes of life, our backs are shaped and strengthened.** In the movie "Shadowlands" we learn about the life of C.S. Lewis and some of the loss that he experienced. The movie culminates with a powerful realization that is spoken by his sweet wife before she dies: **"The pain now is part of the happiness then. That's the deal." This magnificent and perspective-changing idea, if planted within us and given room to grow, can allow us in time to see a "why" in almost any "how?".**

I'm no judge of you. I don't pretend to know or to have felt what you have gone through. I don't assume that the things you have suffered will quickly transform and become a blessing instead of a great curse. **I'm not suggesting that the things that occurred to you have a reason; only that they happened, and because they did, they have now become yours. As the creator that you are, you can now begin to transform them.** I don't have a timeline wherein you have to start feeling and doing better. And yet **I plead with you, as I would plead with myself, to consider the possibility that beyond the great hurt and abuse that you have encountered and suffered, there is power! There is light and a measure of peace! There is the potential for weak things to become strong! I believe it and know it.** Our life has prepared us for this moment; shall we not seize it? Shall we not rise beyond the great valleys of victimization that we are all destined to travel through, and climb the high peaks of this life to regard the wonderful vistas that lie ahead? Shall we not be a blessing unto ourselves, while also liberating and blessing others? Yes, let us take the preparation that has been imparted unto us, and with it change the world!

Life Hack #37
Don't be your own worst critic, be your own best cheerleader.

Chapter 38
Consider all Things

I once met with an individual who was receiving treatment for heroin addiction. He had been through multiple rehabs and had not been able to string together a consistent amount of time wherein he was sober and making positive progress in his life. His life had not been a party; instead, it had been a series of unfortunate events, circumstances, and choices that were constantly contributing to his poisoning. He came to me complaining that he was having a difficult time listening to a staff member in the program because they had not been through what he had been through. He would say, "How can she help me? She hasn't been where I've been—she has no idea what I'm talking about!" After listening to him for a while, I asked him, "Isn't the truth just the truth, regardless of who says it?" Is what an addict or a recovering addict says more true than the words from someone who has never been high, or been dependent? The answer, of course, is no! **We are fools if we refuse to hear truth or wisdom simply because of its source, yet it is so difficult for us to separate the message from the messenger. But if our goal is to be emotionally mature and humble seekers of truth, then our hearts must be soft and willing to hear the truth, regardless of its origin.**

The key word you must adopt and believe in is *consider*. **To** *consider* **simply means to think carefully about something before you make the decision to either agree or disagree with it.** To do this, we must be mind-full instead of brain-full. The brain-full individual immediately accepts or rejects a message simply because it either matches an already existing paradigm or because of the perceived value our brain attaches to the messenger. **To fully** *consider* **the message, we must mind-fully (deliberately) focus on the message and honestly seek for any truth that is present. By** *considering*, **it doesn't mean** that we are obligated to accept; instead, it means that we are committed to examining what has been said, and then to freely and intelligently choose to abide by it, or to simply say, "Thanks, but no thanks."

We get so hung up on, "Well, his tone was just off," or "She's such a hypocrite," or "Why should I do what he says? He never listens to what I say?" We are so narrow-minded! **Are we not all hypocrites? Don't we all fall massively short? Yet when we deal with the world and others in such an entitled and close-hearted way, we become even greater fools by refusing the very truth that can set us free! Just listen to the words, for heaven's sake! Hear them, consider them, and receive from them the value that is there for you.**

This personal philosophy may sound trivial and small, but you will find that there will be times when "considering the message" will require your full, conscious presence, and a deliberate effort to remain mind-full. How much growth do we refuse because of our pride and entitlement? When will we desist in our silly notions that we must only be spoken to in certain ways? When will we decide to let go of our justifications and rationalizations (excuses), and instead open our minds, hearts, and souls to the truth that our friends, parents, teachers, leaders, or strangers have to offer us? **I urge you to seek for truth, so that when it appears in any of its forms (events, circumstances, advice, suggestions, criticism, shouting, soft words), you will be awake, fully conscious, and ready to accept it.**

The Zen proverb "**When the student is ready, the teacher will appear**" speaks to this simple truth. The word "teacher" is metaphorical and does not apply to a single person or entity. Life is a teacher, and so are the infinite circumstances that we must adapt to and grow from. Commit today to being a student—someone who is looking for help and truth! Decide now to consider all things! It is so much easier to live meekly and soft-heartedly than constantly resisting and refusing. During his Sermon on the Mount, Jesus taught, "**Blessed are the meek: for they shall inherit the earth... Blessed are they which do hunger and thirst after righteousness [truth]: for they shall be filled... Blessed are** the pure in heart: for they shall see God." As we open ourselves to learning and being taught, we will indeed find ourselves filled, even overflowing, instead of miserable and wanting. Now go, and *consider*.

Life Hack #38

Take a moment and learn the difference between:
TO, TWO, TOO; YOUR, YOU'RE; THERE, THEY'RE, THEIR; APART, A PART; IT'S, ITS; WHO'S, WHOSE.

Chapter 39
Make Peace with Your Past

It's a necessary part of my profession to travel into the past of people's lives. People come to me emotionally and psychologically trapped and burdened with years of secrets, pain, hurt, disappointments, and abuse, among other things. So much is unresolved! So much of what has happened has left these individuals scared, believing inaccurate things about themselves, about the world, and about others. As they bare their souls and open themselves up to talking and resolving their history, I find that they begin to develop a sense of peace about their past. This is paramount, because **people who are at peace with their past are at peace with their present, and hopeful about their future. Conversely, I find that those who are not at peace with their past are afflicted in the present, and pessimistic about their future.** It's difficult to escape the past untouched, positively or negatively. **We ourselves are a record of our past, with our actions, inactions, circumstances, culture, and beliefs tattooed within our brains and bodies.**

There is a deep need to speak our story. I find that many individuals have an extremely difficult time doing so, and yet, when they do, there is a feeling of liberation that is almost palpable in the room. **As we honestly and fully express the story of our lives, not only is our understanding about ourselves increased, but only then is the unlimited potential for transformation and growth truly unlocked.**

The purpose of this chapter is a call to resolve and find meaning, compassion, and understanding within our past so that it doesn't continue to exert its negative influence upon us. As you search within, you won't have to look far because these are usually the things you remember clearly, yet may have not divulged to anyone. It may have been something you did to someone else or something that was done to you. As you turn your mind to it, you will find that there is a significant amount of energy trapped there, usually in the form of fear, deep hurt, shame, anger, bitterness, regret, and embarrassment. These are the feelings we are looking to release or at least diminish greatly so that they no longer twist our perceptions of ourselves, others, and the world around us. As perceptions change, our feelings change, which in turn makes it that much easier for our behaviors to become congruent with our highest purposes. **I'm not expecting you to feel indifferent or apathetic about your past, only to look at it with more mature and mind-full eyes, in order to resolve the thought patterns, and feeling patterns that are poisoning your present existence.**

For those of you who are carrying these crosses upon your shoulders, I promise that there is relief and an innate ability to move beyond the trauma (inflicted or self-inflicted) that you have been exposed to. **We are made to overcome trauma.** It is natural for us to move beyond those events in our history, many times without any negative consequences at all (often stronger, in fact), and yet there is also the reality that at times people become trapped in their trauma. **The problem with trauma, of course, is that it doesn't just live in the past—it's alive and well inside of you right now, and constantly being fed by the negative emotions and negative thought patterns that continue to provide it air and sustenance.** The purpose is for you to be able to look to your past with your more mature and mind-full eyes, in order to bring compassion and understanding to the events that continue hurting you and distorting your present and future. It's obvious to me that individuals who are burdened with resentment, anger, and fear about their past continue to suffer in the present. Once again, **as you see your past peacefully, you will find that peace will naturally abide in the present moment, and stretch into the future.**

There are really two tracks here. One for those who have perpetrated trauma on or victimized someone, and the other for those who have been victimized by others. Both require healing, and both require confession (the expression of it). The following steps are only made to be signposts, with the realization that as you take action, you will find those events and circumstances changing within you, and working for your benefit.

To those victimized:

- **Express what has occurred to you:** This can first be done individually in the form of writing the event down in your journal. Also, I would highly recommend you express the harm that has been done to you to a spouse, a family member, a religious leader, a therapist, or a friend who is worthy of your trust.

- **As you talk/write about events, notice feelings that are trapped there and seek to resolve and release them:** This is usually done as we reframe and view what has occurred from different perspectives. Many times, those whom we trust this information with can help us to view our circumstances, even ourselves, differently.

- **Move toward forgiveness:** If you feel that forgiveness is not possible at this time, allow at least some room for it inside your heart where, with time, that sentiment may change, grow, and flourish (review the "Forgive" section of Chapter 31 - Apologize and Forgive).

- **Move toward growth and evolution:** I'm a believer that this is indeed one of our greatest gifts—the ability to transform the tragedies of our lives into our greatest achievements; our greatest pain into our most powerful source of wisdom and compassion. Realize that this is possible for you! As you become more and more liberated by those things that have held you captive, your ability to grow and expand will be increased.

To those who have victimized others:

- **Acknowledge what you have done:** If possible, confess this to a therapist, a religious leader, or someone who is worthy of this information. **Remember that it is not the telling that is hard—it is the resistance to telling that creates such suffering within us.**

- **If personal behaviors are still problematic and inflicting harm, work feverishly and with renewed zeal to completely eradicate them from your life:** True healing will occur only as you begin to distance yourself from the behaviors that compromise your highest sense of self.

- **Right the wrong:** When you have reached a more complete understanding of what you have done and the impact of your actions, consider (if possible and appropriate) righting the wrong. You can do this by writing a letter or a message to the individual whom you have harmed or offended. If possible, do it in person. If not, find some other way of communicating to that individual. These moments of humility can be especially healing to those whom you have hurt. **Never underestimate your ability to make things better.** If you cannot right the wrong, then begin to live your life in a way that manifests your change of heart.

- **Move toward forgiveness of yourself and others who may have hurt you:** Your mistakes do not define who you are, and they are certainly not predictors of who you'll become. As you forgive yourself, you allow yourself to move beyond the shame, pain, self-hatred, and negative momentum that your toxic behaviors can create.

- **Move toward growth and evolution:** Make a commitment to move forward and advance in your life. Do so personally and interpersonally. There is no joy in self-neglect. Meaning, purpose, and happiness follow those who, with a sense of gratitude, make use of the gifts and talents they possess for the benefit of all who surround them.

May you find the courage inside to begin the steps I've outlined here. As you do, you may find some internal resistance and increased emotional upset. Some of this is due to the fact that you are finally addressing something you have ignored and avoided. Like Pandora's box, some things are going to leak out that will not feel pleasing. Know this: this does not mean that what you are doing is wrong. Instead, the opposite is true. Trust that the process of acknowledging, expressing, and seeking to understand is incredibly valuable and will change your life if you allow it. I wish you my very best, and may you commit to and trust the process you are about to engage in.

LIFE HACK #39
BE A VOICE, NOT AN ECHO.

CHAPTER 40
SHIFT FROM WANTING TO BE VALUED, TO BEING VALUABLE

While I was vacationing in northern Utah by Bear Lake, I came across a book by Ester Rasband entitled *Confronting the Myth of Self-Esteem.* There were several principles that truly touched me as I read the book, but the one that stayed with me the very most, and which has been invaluable to others, is the **brilliant psychology of shifting your mindset from wanting to be valued by others, to being valuable to others.** Individuals who live by the "I want/need to be valued by others" mantra increase their risk for:

- Emotional instability.

- A constant worry about what others are thinking and feeling about them.

- A feeling of lack of control over their lives and emotions.

- A dependency on others to feel good about themselves and their life.

- A tendency to personalize other people's mistakes by turning them into whether they care OR don't care about them.

In a way, their mantra is, "If you do this, feel this, think this, then that means you care and that I'm valuable. If you don't, it means you don't care, and that I'm not worth caring about." This rollercoaster-like existence of "when others value me I'm valuable and worthwhile" is an incorrect and corrupt psychology, that at some point that individual has adopted. **This obsession about what others are thinking and feeling will invariably lead to an extreme focus on external circumstances, and a lack of awareness and insight on what is happening internally.** This often causes the individual to be critical of others, to blame others for their own emotional state and circumstances, to pressure the people around them to feel in certain ways, and to be overly controlling of their environment and the people around them. This makes good logical sense because these people see their well-being and happiness as originating outside of them. Thus, they will attempt to manage and control the outside environment to feel better.

These individuals are constantly measuring and keeping tabs on whether other people are doing things that show that they value them. Because of their dependence on being valued by others, they will obsess about and engage in mindreading, and jump to assumptions about what other people are feeling about them. This state of dependence will be exacerbated as they become stuck in a negative feedback loop of questions that foster feelings of hopelessness and helplessness. Questions like, "Why doesn't anybody care?" or "Why am I the only one who cares around here?" These dead-end, poisonous questions will further bury the individual in their blindness and helplessness about their life. It's like trying to fill a bucket with a hole in it; the water is always seeping out. **Placing my sense of worth on another's perspective of me is much like placing my sense of worth in relation to the stock market. This "Dow Jones" like existence will often frustrate spouses and friends who wonder, "Will anything ever be enough?!"**

But this isn't a witch hunt! As difficult as these words are to hear for some of you, I don't blame you or condemn you for thinking and feeling this way. I can see how individuals become stuck in this mindset. I get stuck in this type of psychology at times! It's not fun believing and feeling what I've spent three paragraphs explaining. Three things need to happen for people to shift away from this internal corruption.

1. Fully accept the reality that our value as individuals is set to "high." Like a colleague of mine used to say, "God only makes Porsches." **Your worth and value are not variable or dependent on other people's opinions, approval, or even their actions! We are valuable because we are children of God, unlimited, eternal. Not even our scandalous behavior can remove us from this**

standing. Valuable is who I am... it's who you are, too!

2. We need to recognize that our potential is nearly unlimited. This doesn't mean that I can be a Michael Jordan or an Einstein, but that **with focus and attention, we can expand in almost any possible way we choose.** In addition, change can happen in a minute! I've watched individuals make immediate changes that have had a dramatic impact in the totality of their lives.

3. We need to shift our attention and energy to "How can I be valuable to others and the circumstances around me?" Let's get out of the helpless and hopeless pit of "How can I be valued?" and into the empowering philosophy that "**I can be valuable immediately... right now!" You will find, that when you're valuable to others and the circumstances around you, that people will naturally value you more. It's all about the focusing and doing the right things, instead of the wrong things.**

Commit to shifting away from the dependent, erratic, and uncertain philosophy that we must be valued, or that we *deserve* (D-bomb) to be valued! While it may be true that to love and to be loved by others is our most significant spiritual and biological need, chasing it obsessively only creates the opposite outcome. I've found that the more needy someone is, the less likely they are to receive quality love from others. Value from others, much like happiness and peace, must ensue as the natural outcome of living a life that is kind, loving, caring, forgiving, purposeful, and giving. So let's get to it...and start asking and responding to the question, "How can I be valuable, right now?"

LIFE HACK #40
USE DEODORANT. THIS WILL INCREASE YOUR CHANCES OF HAVING & KEEPING FRIENDS.
(MOSTLY FOR YOU BOYS!)

Chapter 41
Meet the Inner Critic

Hey there, loyal friend! Here's something for you. **As a rule, be generous in praise and compliments, and stingy on criticism.** This is a good suggestion on how to treat others, as well as yourself.

The inner critic refers to that part of us that is constantly looking for faults in ourselves and others. In some people, the inner critic is alive and well, while in others he is a bit more subdued. How about for you? Do you spend a lot of time finding fault with others and with yourself? Remember that it isn't just your external behaviors that impact your mood and sense of happiness; **your internal behavior and habits have a tremendous impact on your level of happiness and joy.** As a rule, criticism isn't a positive method of providing feedback to people because it is condemning. Here are a few examples:

- "You never do your dishes" vs. "You didn't do the dishes as I asked."

- "You're no good at math" vs. "You didn't do very well on the last test. I wonder what was difficult for you to understand?"

- "You're not athletic" vs. "That was a tough game. I have some suggestions that may help, can I give them to you?"

- "You're a bad listener" vs. "I noticed that you were distracted today."

You get the idea. Criticism is a faulty method of feedback because it commits three deadly errors.

1. **It generalizes:** The individual who criticizes many times uses words like you *never*, or you *always*. **These generalizing terms are hope-killers because they communicate the message, "You sucked back then,**

you suck now, and you will always suck!" Not a good message and, more importantly, not an accurate description of the problem.

2. **It creates an identity:** Notice that in the criticism, the individual is being attacked, and placed in a category (bad listener, not athletic, not good at math, never does dishes). However, with feedback, it is the *behavior* that is being addressed.

3. **It usually places people on the defense:** Criticism is attacking. As a result, you will find that people will often go on the defensive with you. When we are in defense mode we are usually not very open, which then defeats the purpose of giving feedback, (changing behavior).

I want you to be open. I want you to be open-minded and courageous in the face of criticism and feedback. We are interested in truth when it is spoken to us, regardless of where it is coming from or how it is being delivered. And yet, for you I desire a higher set of skills. A better working model that will yield a better outcome with others and yourself.

More importantly, perhaps, is how you use this skill with yourself. Some people have a very demanding and mean inner critic. This internal voice is punishing, fault-finding, and downright catastrophic. This pattern of thought can be corrosive to the mind-full self. After a while, we begin to believe what the brain-full, critical self is saying about us. These critical thoughts can be in the form of self-hatred, self-disgust, feeling gross, thoughts of being stupid, and thoughts about being a failure. **It's time for a psychological spring cleaning.** It's time to challenge this faulty psychology and replace it with a more accurate and effective personal philosophy.

Do you know what the best part is about the statements above? It's that these self-critical thoughts are untrue! How do I know that? Because I know the truth about who I am, and about who you are! Yes, I do. You are an eternal being of almost unlimited capacity. I know that you are meant to grow, expand, and develop. You will never stop growing! Your mind will never stop pulling you toward self-actualization and joy. Your brain and body are made to learn, adapt, and transform. You are intelligent; thus, you can learn from errors and continue on, wiser than you were just a few minutes ago. Listen to me very closely! **There is nothing that you have done, or could ever do—NOTHING—that merits feelings of self-hatred or self-disgust. If you have made errors, even significant ones, I need you to rise up and go take care of them. I need you to stop what you're doing and get the help that you need. There is always hope, and you can take that to the bank!**

I want you to make a firm commitment to be loyal! I want you to be a loyal friend to yourself and others. **When your brain goes on a fault-finding mission, slow it down a bit, and be gentle with feedback to yourself and others.** Speak the truth sincerely, and yet do it with some class and in a way that will yield a positive outcome. Now go and speak a kind word.

LIFE HACK #41
IF YOU CAN'T IMAGINE 'DROPPING THE MIC' AFTER THE FINAL SENTENCE OF AN ESSAY,
YOUR CONCLUSION NEEDS TO BE STRONGER.

Chapter 42
Time for a Poem

Time for a bit of culture. This specific poem is by Fernando Pessoa, a Portuguese poet, writer, literary critic, translator, publisher and philosopher. He is described as one of the most significant literary figures of the 20th century and one of the greatest poets in the Portuguese language. In my search for amazing material to spoon-feed you, I found this gem. See if you like it. It's called "Rocks along the way."

I may have defects, live anxiously and
sometimes become irritated,
but I never forget that my life is the biggest
enterprise in the world...
and that I can avoid its bankruptcy.

To be happy is to recognize that life is worth living,
even with all its challenges, misunderstandings,
and its periods of crisis.

To be happy, is to stop being the victim of problems
And become the author of your own story.
It is to cross the deserts outside of yourself, and to
find an oasis inside your soul.

It is to thank God each morning for the miracle of life.
To be happy, is not to be afraid of your own emotions.
It is knowing how to speak about yourself.
To have the courage to listen to a "no"!!!
To have the strength to receive a criticism,
even when unjust.

Rocks along the road?
I save them all, one day I'll build a castle...

For me the beauty of this poem lies in the powerful perspective that it encapsulates. What do you like about it? Stay gentle with yourself. Be hopeful. Be brave and use the experiences that are happening for you. Now go and build a castle!

LIFE HACK #42
"NOT BAD" IS NOT GOOD ENOUGH.
RAISE YOUR STANDARD!

CHAPTER 43
3 THINGS I LEARNED FROM A MOUSE

In *The Tale of Despereaux* by Kate DiCamillo, we learn about a young mouse who knew no fear. He was short, had big ears, and no matter how much others attempted to persuade him to feel and act like a mouse, he never did. He lived by a higher set of values. He was a gentleman! Here's what I learned from this small mouse, and perhaps you can learn as well:

1. *"There are those hearts, reader, that never mend again once they are broken. Or if they do mend, they heal themselves in a crooked and lopsided way, as if sewn together by a careless craftsman. Such was the fate of Chiaroscuro. His heart was broken. Picking up the spoon and placing it on his head, speaking of revenge, these things helped him to put his heart together again. But it was, alas, put together wrong."* There is a point in the story when one of the characters (Chiaroscuro), is making a sincere effort to do something right and it goes terribly wrong. His heart breaks, and as a result he becomes very angry, bitter, and vengeful. Sometimes this happens to us. We begin with good intentions, wanting to do the right thing, but the result is disappointing, or painful. This heartbreak can become toxic and poison us, turning what was once lovely and kind to fearful and angry. **Remember that the good you do is sufficient. The kindness you give stands by itself and does not need to be recognized. The love you offer is a gift to the world. The forgiveness you render to others does not need recognition. Keep your heart soft, hopeful, and giving.**

2. *"The story is not a pretty one. There is violence in it. And cruelty. But stories that are not pretty have a certain value, too, I suppose. Everything, as you well know (having lived*

in this world long enough to have figured out a thing or two for yourself), cannot always be sweetness and light." As I have stated before, this life is the complete package! It is bitterness and sweet, light and darkness, love and fear, all packaged up tightly in burrito-like fashion. **Don't ever judge this life, or make choices based on what is easy or hard. Easy and hard aren't facts, they are opinions. Don't look for *easy*, look for meaningful. Don't blame *hard*, become better instead.**

3. *"Forgiveness, reader, is, I think, something very much like hope and love—a powerful, wonderful thing. And a ridiculous thing, too. Isn't it ridiculous, after all, to think that a son could forgive his father for beating the drum that sent him to his death? Isn't it ridiculous to think that a mouse ever could forgive anyone for such perfidy? But still, here are the words Despereaux Tilling spoke to his father. He said, "I forgive you, Pa." And he said those words because he sensed it was the only way to save his own heart, to stop it from breaking in two. Despereaux, reader, spoke those words to save himself."* This world is in desperate need of forgiveness. I urge you to become the type of person that is secure, loving, and mature enough to forgive others for their ignorance, folly, and wrongs. **Are we not all stained and deeply in need of forgiveness ourselves?** Keep your heart whole, and freely give the gift of forgiveness.

LIFE HACK #43
THE EASY ROAD USUALLY LEADS TO THE BOTTOM, SO...
TAKE THE HIGH ROAD.

Chapter 44
On Suicide

Just yesterday a young man who lived in my community committed suicide. He left a video on Facebook as a note, giving a reason for the action he later took. He didn't want anyone to feel blame. He attempted to reassure others it wasn't about them, only that he didn't really know why, but he couldn't go on. He thought that perhaps he was mentally ill, but either way, it was too much. He seemed kind and considerate. He was bright. He appeared sincere and didn't want to hurt anyone. He apologized to friends and said goodbye to them. He wrote notes to some of them. He addressed his mother, father, and siblings in the hope that what he was considering doing wouldn't be taken personally or be damaging to them. He was trying to be real. He was like you. He was like all of us. We all need a boy like that to live!

Can I be real with you? I began this book with a promise that I would be absolutely honest, and not treat you like a child; that I would speak clearly, and give you the very best that I possess...well, here it goes! I feel for this young man. I feel for his brothers and his family as well. I feel for his friends. The young man in this message was not well. He felt hopeless, and was convinced that he was helpless. He seemed sure that this was the only option, the only possible way...but I have to tell you, he was incorrect. I wrote this book with the hope that those who read it would realize that there is great suffering in this world, and yet that there is an even greater hope and, more importantly, we are the carriers of that hope. He was a carrier of that hope as well. It's obvious that there was great suffering in this young man, perhaps the greatest type of suffering. I refer to the suffering that is loneliness, and feelings of being unloved. But suffering is never just suffering. Suffering never travels alone, it always brings two things with it...hopelessness and the truth. **What is the truth? The truth is something that this**

young man now understood. He now knew deep inside of him, in the way that perhaps only those who feel neglected truly know, that to live is to be a carrier of hope and love. This is the ultimate goal of living. If the hurt and rejection of this world have brought you to this place, it is a gift, one that you must now utilize to bring redemption and love to others.

You are meant for great things! Your life is uniquely significant. Your presence, your friendship, your intelligence, your experience is deeply needed in this world. Not one other person is you. No one can say what you say in the way you say it. No one laughs the way you laugh. No one can lift others the way you lift them. No one smiles quite like you smile. No one can speak about your personal struggles the way you do. Only you. **I need you to live! Perhaps I'm selfish in saying it; so be it, but your unique life experience is necessary.**

I can understand that the thought of your suffering and frustration with life coming to an end can feel like relief. I can even understand that suicide may feel like your only viable option to escape your circumstances. May I be so bold, and I say this in the kindest tone I can muster, to suggest that suicide is not the answer for you? **Living is the choice for you! And not just living, but living large! And not only living, but bringing life to others as well. You can become the bringer of light. Perhaps your mission is revealing itself to you this very moment. Sometimes it is only in the darkest of nights that we can see the complete brightness and beauty of the stars.**

There is hope! There is life! There are kisses to be given. Hugs to be had. Children to be born! Miracles to be seen, and in which you will have a hand. **The world needs your hands. It needs your wisdom and clarity. It needs your struggle.**

You and I may not know each other, but I'm connected to you. My children are connected to you. Like ripples in the water, our influence impacts the collective conscience and experience we inhabit. **I summon your courage. I call for your compassion. I invoke your highest reason and logic, not only to stay, but to stay and engage life in a new way!**

Reach upward! Reach outward! The moment has arrived. It is a turning point in your life. It's time for you to share your moment with others. It's time for you to rise from the ashes like a phoenix! Even now, as you pass through the valley of the shadow of death, a new life awaits you. You can't go back to things the way they were—really, you can't. A new phase is starting for you.

There are moments in our life that change us forever. Perhaps this is one of those moments. **As you rise from the rubble of your struggles, I promise you, you will find diamonds—even a new and more complete perspective. Remember that no failure is terminal. No emotion is chronic. No situation final. Life is in constant flux, and you—you can change course. You can try new and different things.** Small steps and small changes can yield huge outcomes. My friend, be patient. Emotions change, situations transform, and somehow in the midst of all that change lies peace and wisdom. It is there like a treasure and perhaps, with a little bit of guidance, you can uncover it and become a richer individual and live a fuller life.

You may need some help. You may require another's strength and perspective. **You may need someone else's light to light your way for a moment, but soon enough yours will burn brightly, and before you know it, you will become a source of light for others. Don't feel bad asking for help—we all need help. It is in helping and receiving help that we heal from the wounds of this world.**

Your courage inspires my courage. Your compassion motivates my compassion. Your wisdom enhances my wisdom. Your joy brings joy. Your heart is soft, your mind is willing. Instead of a suicide note, write a new beginnings letter. Instead of reaching for death, reach for a friend, and reach for help. Perhaps someday we will meet. You can share your experience with me, and together we will rejoice as friends. Your life will fill mine, and mine yours. My friend... stay!

Life Hack #44
It's hard to feel good about yourself
if you haven't done anything worth feeling good about.

CHAPTER 45
MIND YO' BUSINESS

It's going to be a lovely day, isn't it? I remember reading Byron Katie's book *Loving What Is* a few years back, and coming upon this gem that she shared in her book. Here are some of her words:

"I can find only three kinds of business in the universe: mine, yours, and God's. *For me, the word God means 'reality.' Reality is God, because it rules. Anything that's out of my control, your control, and everyone else's control—I call that God's business.*

"Much of our stress comes from mentally living out of our own business. When I think, 'You need to get a job, I want you to be happy, you should be on time, you need to take better care of yourself,' I am in your business. When I'm worried about earthquakes, floods, war, or when I will die, I am in God's business.

"If you are living your life and I am mentally living your life, who is here living mine? We're both over there. Being mentally in your business keeps me from being present in my own. I am separate from myself, wondering why my life doesn't work. *To think that I know what's best for anyone else is to be out of my business. Even in the name of love, it is pure arrogance, and the result is tension, anxiety, and fear.* **Do I know what's right for me? That is my only business. Let me work with that before I try to solve your problems for you. If you understand the three kinds of business enough to stay in your own business, it could free your life in a way that you can't even imagine."**

It's simple and brilliant, right? This is a wonderful thing to begin teaching your brain. Gently remind your brain where your focus and attention should be. When your brain starts traveling to unknown places (projecting into the future), mind-reading what other people are thinking about you, catastrophizing about the future, or constantly judging and condemning others for what they are doing or not doing, realize that you have already left your own business, and are now living in somebody else's business. The outcome will be frustration, dissatisfaction, anger, and a sense of helplessness ("Things are out of my control!"no duh!). **If you arrive at this place, far away from where your attention should really be, laugh out loud (or silently if you wish—don't want people thinking you're crazy...wait, that's not my business) and remind yourself to return back to where your power really lies.**

It's important to note that I'm not suggesting you become completely self-involved, uncaring, or that you simply disregard others. It's of critical importance to know how to reach for others, and how to do so in the most effective way. Perhaps you can read this small chapter in conjunction with Chapter 10 (3 Questions You Must Master) and Chapter 3 (The Beam in Your Eye). The key word here is "influence." Our reach and influence can only go so far. **I always describe advice giving as a gift that you offer and then let go of and allow the recipient the freedom to do with it what they will. Remember that your life is the greatest and most important enterprise, and that you must care for it with utmost attention, encouragement, and compassion.**

To recap, let's return to Byron Katie:"The next time you're feeling stress or discomfort, ask yourself whose business you're in mentally, and you may burst out laughing! That question can bring you back to yourself. And you may come to see that you've never really been present, that you've been mentally living in other people's business all your life. Just to notice that you're in someone else's business can bring you back to your own wonderful self." Remember to MYOB (Mind Your Own Business).

LIFE HACK #45
NEVER SUPPRESS A GENEROUS THOUGHT.

CHAPTER 46
"I'M NOT THROWIN' AWAY MY SHOT"

I don't know when you will pick up this book, or when you will read this specific chapter, but as I write this, the musical *Hamilton* has taken the world by storm. A powerful true story, with great music, amazing lyrics, and the freedom and independence of the United States of America as a backdrop...the combination is MONEY (as we used to say in the nineties)!! I first became aware of the musical as my wife and children became absolutely obsessed with its music. Lin Manuel Miranda (author and lyricist) took an extraordinary life and story and put it to hip-hop/rap to generate one of the most outstanding and memorable plays ever made. The music is full of small passages that beg to be repeated by me, and learned by you.

The play follows the life of Alexander Hamilton as he joins the revolution against British rule and the ultimate independence of the United States. His story teaches us that **good things come to those who wait, but great things come to those invest relentlessly.** Hamilton apparently was that kind of individual. Here are five of my favorite inspirational quotes from the musical:

1. **"I am not throwin' away my shot."** Hamilton was wonderful example of someone who took advantage of what was in front of him. He saw the opportunity and he seized it. He wasn't afraid of failure; he understood that **risk is a necessary part of creation.** Look around you. **Don't look for what you don't have. Stop complaining about what's missing.** Stop comparing, as if what others have could somehow devalue you. Don't waste your time complaining that life is hard. Don't throw away the goodness that is in front of you. **If it's hard, try harder and smarter!** If you don't understand something, ask for help. If your school offers clubs, sports, plays, groups, extra-curricular activities, music, art, etc., pick one or two and go

for it. Don't waste your shot because of insecurity or because you're not good at something. Of course you're not good at it—you haven't spent countless hours doing it—yet! Instead, think like Hamilton: **"I'm past patiently waitin'. I'm passionately smashin' every expectation. Every action's an act of creation! I'm laughin' in the face of casualties and sorrow. For the first time, I'm thinkin' past tomorrow"**!

2. **"History has its eyes on you."** Indeed it does. The things you do and value will have a tremendous impact on your life. I understand where some of you have come from. I understand that all of you in some small or large way have gone through some difficult and disappointing times, and yet **your history beckons you, calls to you, begs you to live honorably.** Live with class. Bring something to the table. Your voice matters. **Your words matter. With one word, you can change the mood in a room. That's powerful!** The opinions you have about things are of critical importance; it's time to stand for the things that are of greatest worth. **Quit spending hours being entertained, and start creating. Stop being a taker, and become a giver, and a builder. Live your life in a manner that your children would be proud of. Live in an exemplary way—a way that can be emulated. Yes, your actions of today will become history later…so make it an awesome history!**

3. **"Young, scrappy and hungry."** You gotta stay hungry! Part of my own challenge, and perhaps yours, is that life has put us to sleep. We are living our lives unconsciously. Routines often do this to us. **We mindlessly float along with the current and end up in the middle of the ocean, with no land and no direction in sight. We are not dogs waiting for a bell to ring so we can go and claim what is ours—we have to go and get it!** You have to stay hungry. You have to take the front row seat; you have to raise your hand; you have to have an opinion. I envy you.

There is an energy in youth that is electric. I feel it every time I am with you. Every time I walk into a school, I sense it. It is contagious! Remember that, as *Hamilton*'s Aaron Burr proclaims, "I am the one thing in life I can control, I am inimitable, I am an original." **Write your story, claim your birthright, and go get what's yours.**

4. **"It might be nice, it might be nice, to have Washington on your side."** General George Washington makes his way on the scene as the leader of the Revolutionary Army. His presence and moral courage ultimately lead the rebel forces to victory. As a result he becomes a revered and respected force. This quote is all about having the right people in your corner. Think of your own life and the people in it. Who would be nice to have on your side? Teachers, parents, siblings, religious leaders, coaches, business owners, other people of influence? Look, you don't have to do everything on your own in life. **Don't burn bridges—build them and nurture them. An emotionally secure and enlightened individual not only seeks the advice of others, but looks to improve his relationships with those people.** I'm sure you've heard the quote, **"It's not what you know, it's who you know."** I think you'll find that as the years pass, and you look back through your life, you'll be surprised how true this little saying is. Want good grades in school? Make friends with your teachers. Want a great home life? Build and nurture your relationships with your parents and siblings. Want to have a great time at school and in life? Join groups, clubs, teams, and religious groups that give you a wide and powerful swath of individuals who have your back, and who are connected. Build, build, build, and get the very best people you can on your side.

5. **"Rise up! Wise up! Eyes up!"** I love it. This is a maxim for life, isn't it? I love that you are reading this book. **I applaud you because you, like Alexander Hamilton, "got a lot of brains, but no polish...you're a diamond**

in the rough, a shiny piece of coal." By investing in this book, in education, in arts, in sports, and in everything that is inspiring, you are wising up. **Keep your eyes up, your back straight, your chin up. Smile, bring a pleasant disposition to those around you.** Look to mentors, to teachers, to those worthy of emulation. Look up to God. Rise up! Wise up! Eyes up!

LIFE HACK #46
EVERY DAY WRITE DOWN THREE THINGS YOU'RE GRATEFUL FOR AND WHY.

CHAPTER 47
POOR, GOOD, BETTER, BEST

Hey, welcome back. Time to wise up; hear me out. There are so many choices to make in this life. Some will appear to have a tremendous influence, others will seem inconsequential. Either way, let me give you a bit of a working model to help you enhance your choice making. **In the great laboratory of life, you are the scientist. Your job is to gain the best spiritual, psychological, and educational information, and then apply it in your decision making.**

I think you and I can agree that there are some choices in this life that are just poor. Poor because they cause harm to us or to others. Poor because they fill us with resentment, bitterness, anger, entitlement, and blame. Poor because they steal hope and replace it with indifference. Poor because the outcome or fruit of those choices is not congruent with your highest values and aspirations. Here are some examples: lying, cheating, stealing, gossiping, blaming others, being overly critical, sex, drugs, pornography, manipulation, nude pictures (requesting or taking them), isolating from others, being rude, disrespectful, unforgiving—you get the point. **As a scientist, you can see that these choices are poor because they are based on inferior psychology, and because they produce faulty outcomes.** Toss them to the trash heap!

Now, the lines between good, better, and best choices are a bit more difficult to distinguish than the line between poor and good choices, but remember that the subtitle of this book, and your ultimate goal, is to live an awesome life. For that to happen, you must possess an awesome psychology, and your actions and choices must be awesome as well. **One of the purposes of this life is to uncover those things that are of most worth and value. It is those things that you want to place in the better and best categories, and thus position them as high priority items**. Those things that will create the highest levels of friendship, meaning, achievement, experience, honor, love, and joy are the ones that we want to invest most of our time in. Here are some fun examples:

- Posting gossip: poor. Looking at Instagram: good. Texting a friend: better. Hanging out with a friend: best.

- Isolating in your room: poor. Being around family or friends: good. Laughing, interacting, and being complimentary of others: better and best.

- Being unkind to parents and siblings: poor. Being civil to parents and siblings: good. Helping, complimenting, and showing interest in their lives: better and best.

- Dropping out of school: poor. Attending school: good. Being engaged, using your teachers as a resource, and working your little tail off: better and best.

- Using your phone to view pornography, spread gossip, or as a time suck: poor. Using your phone as healthy entertainment: good. Using your phone as a tool to connect to others: better. Using your phone as a tool to organize your life, and to inspire yourself and others: best.

You get the idea. Like Ice-T (old rapper dude) used to say, **"Check yourself before you wreck yourself!"** Use this little scale to measure your choices, and then make a shift from spending your time in poor and good activities, and begin to migrate your choosing toward better and best.

LIFE HACK #47
TOUCHING SOMEONE'S SHOULDER OR ARM WHILE ASKING THEM OUT
HAS BEEN PROVEN TO INCREASE THEIR CHANCES OF SAYING "YES."

Chapter 48
On Divorce

Watch out—things are about to get serious. This is not an easy topic to write about, but it is very necessary. There's a chance that some of you reading this book come from divorced homes. I don't know your circumstances and, honestly, I don't need to know them. I myself experienced divorce at the age of 11. It's difficult to have your dream, or your idea of what your family was going to be, die. It's a tragedy, really, one of enormous proportions. It can be very disheartening as a child to see your parents falter and make poor decisions. I've seen respect die in the hearts of adolescents, only to be replaced by indifference and anger.

Sometimes this already difficult time can become even more challenging with the introduction of a step-parent or step-brothers and sisters. Sometimes there are custody and visitation issues, and even though parents are divorced, they continue to fight. Perhaps the most tragic of circumstances is when parents, in their own blindness and ignorance, place you in the middle of that conflict. They speak rudely about the other parent and berate them in front of you. What is to be done? Is there something you *can* do? Will it ever get better?

I have some thoughts for you. I want you to consider them, and if you feel they are reasonable and logical, perhaps apply them in your own life.

1. **Parents are human:** We are all a little crazy, and some of us face significant challenges. These challenges sometimes rob us of precious awareness. **It is in this mind-less and lost state that parents can at times act out in tragic ways.** They can become abusive, disloyal, defensive, attacking, bitter, and vengeful. But I have hope for your parents, just like I have hope for mine. It's possible for them to come to themselves again and behave in ways that make

you proud. Sometimes our anger and disappointment make it difficult to give parents a second (or third or fourth) chance. I'm hoping that you and your parents can find a way back to gratitude, appreciation, and love. **Be patient with them.**

2. **Get out of the middle:** Sometimes parents, out of their own insecurity, or because they want to gain your approval and support, will attempt to pit you against the other parent. This is very unfortunate. First of all let me say, **your heart is big enough to love two individuals who don't presently like each other.** This is true! Second, I'm going to ask you to be brave; respectfully, but directly, tell your parent that you don't want to be placed in this position. Like this: "Mom/Dad, I don't like it when you speak badly about Mom/Dad. Please don't do it around me." "Mom/Dad, I love the both of you. I'm not interested in picking between you. Please don't guilt me for visiting the other." "Mom/Dad, if you have concerns or complaints about Mom/Dad, please talk to them about it, and not me. Thank you."

3. **Divorce is not the end:** This may be the most difficult one for you, because you may be thinking that no good can possibly come from this, and that it can't possibly get better. My dear friend, you are wiser and better than that thinking. **Your ability to digest an experience, and metabolize it into something meaningful and life-changing is among your most remarkable strengths.** Remember the words of John Patrick: **"Pain makes men think; thinking makes men wise; and wisdom makes living exciting, beautiful, hopeful and joyful."** I don't wish for your suffering any more than I wished for mine. But it is here! It is at the doors, is it not? **Shall we not learn from the struggle and suffering of others? Shall we not become wiser because of their folly? Shall we not be more consciously prepared to avoid the icebergs that dot our horizons?** Yes, we will, and we must.

4. **Don't let these events poison you:** I've met many of you who, because of the divorce of your parents, have sworn off having families, marrying, or even believing in love. May I just say, it wasn't love that broke them apart! **Don't confuse the beauty and purity of love with blindness and selfishness.** Call it what it is! **You must not allow the tragedy of your past to become the fear of, and hopelessness about, the future. Your future awaits the choices of today.** Be loving, be giving, be loyal, be forgiving! Yes, bad things can happen, even terrible things, but those must never override the life-giving principles that you can adopt at this moment. **Consciously work to transform your tragedy into a commitment to being better.**

5. **Don't add to the fire:** Divorce can overwhelm us. It can derail us. Perhaps you feel numb, as if the experience is surreal. Maybe you feel angry and hurt. Some feel lost, unsure and disconnected. Regardless of what you feel (and what you feel is legitimate and important), I'm here to coach you. I'm here to ask something extremely difficult of you: **I'm going to ask you to raise your game.** I'm going to ask you to be a bit more mind-full and, as a result, I want you to be a blessing in your home, to your parents, and to your siblings. "Iuri, are you freaking crazy?" "Hmm...come on, now, you know I'm completely out of my mind!" Yes, I'm going to ask you to not add to the already burning fire that is scorching the ground beneath you. **I want you to be a relief. I want you to be a source of kindness. A listening ear.** You may need some help doing this. You may need your friends, a counselor, or a wise religious leader. **Asking for help is normal. Anyone who has any intelligence at all knows that we can function a bit better with the help of others.** My friend, the lesson you must learn today is this: **your relationships will be the things that demand the very best of you in your life.** Begin today. Don't worry about what has been done or what

has been said—it's time to switch sails, turn the rudder, and head toward softer seas. My best to you.

I want you to know that I'm cheering for you from the sidelines. I'm the scandalous one with the ridiculous mustache and your name painted on my bare chest (this is an unfortunate image). Go forward, my friend. Step with courage. Decide today that with you things will be different. That you will learn from the unfortunate choices of others. Don't turn to drugs, alcohol, or pornography! Don't add more suffering to your life. Don't become unconscious, for heaven's sake! **Pick a joyful spot in the horizon, and fearlessly begin the journey.**

Life Hack #48

"WHEN YOU MEET SOMEONE, TREAT THEM AS IF THEY ARE IN SERIOUS TROUBLE, AND YOU WILL BE RIGHT MORE THAN HALF OF THE TIME."

-Henry B. Eyring

Chapter 49
Don't Fake it 'Til You Make it

I'm stepping into dangerous territory here. I've decided to go against Master Yoda to insist that there is such a thing as "try!" If you are not a Star Wars geek, you may not be familiar with Yoda's famous statement, "Do or do not, there is no try!" I still love Master Yoda, so let me present you with this simple idea.

Recently I met with a young woman who was in the midst of a depressive episode. We were discussing the symptoms she was experiencing, and as we began to talk about how to improve her mood, her thinking, and her actions, she stated, "I just don't think I could put on a smile and do all of these things. I would feel like I'm faking it." **It's an interesting thing that happens with individuals who are suffering with depression or other disorders; they begin to believe they *are* the disorders. In other words, they begin to identify with the disorder. They feel that depression, sadness, isolation, a sad affect, a lack of action, is who they are. They feel a sense of loyalty to the emotions they are feeling, to the point that trying something different feels like a betrayal of who they are.** As we discussed the issue and I helped her change her relationship to her thoughts and feelings, she was able to at least psychologically disconnect from the idea that she had to do and be who her thoughts and feelings were saying she was. Also, she was able now to "try" to do things that were congruent with her highest goals and aspirations in life.

I'm also reminded of a young man who reported to me that it was hard for him to feel love for his family and for his siblings. Like the young woman, he was afraid that displaying love and affection to his family would be a betrayal of his feelings. Once he understood that love, as with most things, is on a continuum and that he has the ability to influence where love is on that continuum, he began to feel some hope. **In addition, as he came to realize that being loving and choosing to love is more important than the feeling of being in love, he felt free to try, and was no longer stuck behind a false feeling that he was betraying himself by loving his family.**

I guess I've always had a struggle with the expression, "Fake it 'til you make it." I'm a word guy. **I believe that words are powerful, and if they don't represent reality, then I try to stop saying them. I don't fake it 'til I make it because I don't identify personally with my struggles. I don't believe they are who I am, and they are certainly not a total representation of what I can become. Trying to move forward is not faking! Moving in the direction of my goals and aspirations is not faking! Attempting to fulfill my purpose is not faking!** Showering, cleaning my room, exercising, going for a walk, reaching out to family, becoming engaged in reading a book, showing love to my family and friends, being kind, asking for help, helping a friend or family member is not faking. That is who I am, and most certainly who I am attempting to be! Stop believing that when you are doing things that are congruent with your higher self, you are faking, because it just simply isn't true. **If you feel sad, you don't have to *do* sad! If you feel angry, you don't have to *do* angry! If you are feeling fearful, you don't have to *do* fear!** Don't get me wrong—I'm not implying that it's easy, only that it is possible for you to "try" to do something else without feeling guilty that you are attempting to move in a positive direction. **There is no loyalty in self-loathing! Create positive movement in your life! Pick a direction, any direction, and take a step or two. Anything that you feel is positive, healthy, helpful, and valuable—create some movement in that direction.** Remember that sometimes you smile because you're happy, and other times you're happy because you smile. Isn't it lovely that you can stop faking, and finally just get to work, free of twisted and erroneous thinking? Now let's get to it!

Life Hack #49
Don't post late at night.
Allow the light of day to clear your mind
before you enshrine yourself on social media.

CHAPTER 50
Know Thy Selfie

People are always looking for who they really are. "I'm going to find myself...find out who I really am." The answer or answers to that question are not complicated, but somehow we want to find something deeper and more complex. It feeds our egos a bit to discover something unique that we can wear like a trophy. I believe in spiritual beginnings; namely, that we are spiritual children of a divine being whose heart and purpose are set upon us, and that as children of that loving God, our birthright (should we claim it) is to be partakers of the divine nature, and ultimately to be heirs to all that He has. **Truly, our value is great and potentially unlimited.** Whether we look through the lens of reincarnation, or to more organic and non-spiritual beginnings, we eventually ask the same questions and are forced to either believe in or decide who we are, and who we will become. **Let me suggest a simple truth that seems to run across all beliefs: we are evolving!** We are constantly growing, and if we possess a gentle and truthful philosophy, that growth will promote peace, joy, love, compassion, and a mature responsibility to contribute. Physically, intellectually, spiritually, emotionally, we are made to evolve, and most often do so without any effort on our part. And yet, **unconscious growth will only take us so far, and at times, our environment, family of origin, and history will impose upon us a variety of philosophies and ideologies that are simply untrue, and which can be incredibly corrosive to the divine that is within us**.

One of the purposes of this book is to present you with information that will allow you to see life in its fullness and to better utilize its opportunities. I hope you discover the constant beauty and magnificence that surround you. **I hope you come to love people, as well as yourself. As you begin to view who you**

174

are, and as you recognize yourself as an evolving being, everything then becomes part of that growth. **Our failures, misfortunes, successes, and other experiences all begin to carry within them the seeds of wisdom, redemption, depth, strength, and power.** Imbued with this enlightened understanding, you are able to be more accepting of where you are. **You will find purpose in what once seemed meaningless.** What once irritated you now becomes your classroom. What you once took offense to and resisted now becomes a potential source of light and truth. **The great fear that paralyzes us becomes overwhelmed by the self-evident hope that resides just beyond it. Pain itself transforms.** C.S. Lewis wrote, **"We can ignore even pleasure. But pain insists upon being attended to. God whispers to us in our pleasures, speaks in our conscience, but shouts in our pains: it is his megaphone to rouse a deaf world."**

As unbearable as physical, emotional, and mental pain can be, resisting it, avoiding it, being ashamed of it only seems to magnify it. **Radical acceptance of things as they are, and the search for starlight in the midst of the darkest night, may yet be the greatest of mankind's achievements.** As a result of this change in philosophy, depression and anxiety become messages to us, telling us to stop and take a closer look. A message that something is not right, that something needs to be attended to and resolved. As we stop avoiding and begin sitting with these difficult emotions, we will find that entwined in them are the erroneous ideologies that must be transformed if peace is to ensue. **Let the evolution begin!**

LIFE HACK #50
DON'T WORRY ABOUT WHAT PEOPLE THINK, JUST WORRY ABOUT PEOPLE.

Awesome Advice About Love & Friendship

Chapter 51
To Choose and to Be Chosen

Hey, I've got some news for you! Get ready for some heartbreak. "Come on, Iuri, I was having a really nice day!" "Yeah, whatever...." Okay, let's talk for a moment. I don't know how old you are. I don't know if you've had a boyfriend or girlfriend. To be honest, I don't really care. Okay, I do a little bit, but here is the truth: you will likely experience heartbreak in your life. And when I say heartbreak, I mean the feelings you experience when you begin to really like someone, and they just don't like you back. This may even happen during one of your junior high romances! Yes, it's true. **People change their minds, their feelings change, and what they once liked, even loved, moves and shifts. I'm here to tell you that this is normal.** Remember, these are your dating and getting-to-know people years, not your I'm- ready-to-settle-down-and-start-a-family years. I'm also here to tell you what my wise mother told me many years ago: "Iuri, you don't stay in a dating relationship with people out of obligation! You stay because this person inspires you, and because you love them." If you are staying in a relationship because you are afraid of how your boyfriend/ girlfriend is going to feel if you break up with them, you are there out of obligation, and it's time to mature up and leave the poor sucker. "Iuri, you are cruel!" "It's possible, it's possible, but I don't think so—hear me out!"

I believe that your job is to choose the very best person you want to be with. I also believe that it is your partner's job to pick whomever they believe is the very best for them. So if your girlfriend breaks up with you, yes, you will experience heartbreak, but at least you will intellectually understand that she is doing exactly what she needs to be doing, which is, she is choosing whomever she believes is the very best for them...and apparently, it's not you! I know this reality check may not help you to feel any better, but dang it, it's the truth, and you and I have an agreement to speak the truth at all costs, and to deal in truth, do we not? I feel for you, I really do!

I've shared this with you in previous chapters, but **we do not— we cannot—stay with someone because they are threatening suicide, cutting, causing harm, or any other form of emotional manipulation. This is a clear signal to you that this individual is not well enough to be in a healthy relationship.** Be honorable, have class, and say goodbye. I mean it! I know you're going to rationalize and tell yourself that you are the only one that can help, and that he/she has no one else. Look, I seriously hear you, but the solution isn't for you to stay in a relationship that you don't want to be in, and to remain with someone that is not inspiring or worthy of emulation, and that you are not in love with. I'm sure he/she needs help, so be a dear friend and point them in that direction, but that direction is not back into an unhealthy relationship with you. **We don't stay in relationships out of pity.**

So when heartbreak comes, and you get passed over, cry your tears, reach out to your friends, tell your parents, write in your journal, plead with God even, but intellectually and logically know that the other person is doing exactly what they should be doing, and that maybe they'll miss out on being with someone as amazing as you! See you sucka!

Life Hack #51
If you have to choose between being liked or being respected, choose being respected.

CHAPTER 52

WHAT IS LOVE?

Aaahh, c'est l'amour! Yes, I speak French, but I'm not great at it. Shall we talk love? **If there is a purpose in this life, then it is to learn to love and to be loved.** There is no feeling, choice, or action that is more worthwhile and powerful than love. Why talk about love? As with all things, **I find that as our understanding of things is deepened, so is our ability to utilize those things for our benefit, and for the benefit of those around us.**

Is love merely a feeling? Is it a choice? Is it an action? Can it be influenced, or is it just something that our heart chooses? Is it divine, or is it purely a biological drive for the sake of reproduction and survival of the species? Is love something we fall into, and by implication, something we fall out of?

Take the man who comes to therapy unsure whether he still loves his wife. Does he think love is a feeling or a choice? Is it something that he can nurture, or something that's out of his control and influence?

Perhaps you have had the honor of experiencing a deep feeling of love and affection for someone. Perhaps you have been the recipient of someone's love. It's easy to see why poets, artists, and every possible magazine talks about love, and where to get it. **Nothing fills the human soul with greater happiness than the love, intimacy, and acceptance of another. It's magical, transforming, and enlightening.** And yet, I find that our relationship with love can be misunderstood, and that can lead to intense pain. I remember listening to a talk by Stephen Covey, where he introduced the idea of viewing love not just as an emotion, but as an action. He tells the story of a father who was struggling with his son. The son was making some questionable choices, being disrespectful, and rebelling. Mr. Covey told the gentleman to love his son, to which the dad responded, "Yes, yes, I love him." Mr. Covey repeated the message, "No, you need to love him." "Yes, yes, I love him very much," the man assured him. Mr. Covey then said, "No you don't understand...**you need to be loving to him in your actions, in your attitude, in your words and desires for him." The gentleman understood the message and realized, perhaps for the first time, that love is not just something you feel, but something you invite, promote, and do.**

It's wonderful when, on a scale of 0 to 10, our emotional love tank is running in the high eights, or even in the nines or higher. When we are up that high, being loving is easy—it's natural, it flows freely. But what happens when our emotional love tank is running along in the fives or fours, or threes, or even lower? Is it still possible to be loving? **Can I nurture love by simply being loving? The answer is a resounding yes! It is in these very instances that love is a choice, and what a beautiful and wise choice it is. You can choose love during the moments that your brain and body are hurting. When your brain and body feels disrespected, disappointed and offended! When they (you) feel taken advantage of and scared. When they sound the alarm for you to run, or to protect yourself and fight. It is here that you must believe in love, not just as the emotion that comes upon us, but as our best hope and salvation.** It is here where to be loving will demand the very best of you psychologically, emotionally, spiritually, and physically. It is during these moments that the mind-full and spirit-full us must override our flesh, and fulfill our purpose.

I remember meeting a young couple who were struggling through a difficult time. I remember the young lady asking me, "Why would I be loving and kind, just to get hurt again?" This, of course, is a legitimate question. She had been hurt deeply by something that was done to her, and yet, if her desire was to build the relationship and move forward, then there was no other choice but to be loving. C.S. Lewis, in his book *The Four Loves*, states, **"To love is to be vulnerable. Love anything and your heart will be wrung and possibly broken. If you want to make sure of keeping it**

intact you must give it to no one, not even an animal. Wrap it carefully round with hobbies and little luxuries; avoid all entanglements. Lock it up safe in the casket or coffin of your selfishness. But in that casket, safe, dark, motionless, airless, it will change. It will not be broken; it will become unbreakable, impenetrable, irredeemable. To love is to be vulnerable."

Scott Peck, the author of *The Road Less Traveled*, describes love in this way: "love is the will to extend one's self for the purpose of nurturing one's own or another's spiritual growth. When we grow it is because we are working at it, and we are working at it because we love ourselves. It is through love that we elevate ourselves. And it is through our love for others that we assist others to elevate themselves. **Love, the extension of the self, is the very act of evolution. It is evolution in progress. The evolutionary force, present in all of life, manifests itself in mankind as human love. Among humanity love is the miraculous force that defies the natural law of entropy."** Here Peck describes love not only as the evolutionary force which calls us to elevate others, but also to elevate and nurture ourselves. **Love is the most effective instrument we have to reach one another because love resonates deeply within the divine in us.** It is this kind of love that passes all understanding and rises above circumstance that we must aspire to have within our breast, while rooting out the petty, provincial, and conditional flesh that haunts us even now.

*To love is to stay and to leave. To love is to be kind and to confront. To love is to speak and to hold your peace. It is to promote peace and go to war. It is to rescue and to allow suffering. It is to hold and let go. It is to share and keep close. It is to move and stand still. It is to rise and stay low. To try and fail, and then try again! It is to rejoice and suffer long. It is to be just and merciful. It is to stand hurt, disappointed, betrayed, offended, unsure, and to move with faith, **knowing that perfect love never fails to plant the seed of hope, or to promote and invite the divine within us.*** Love is less about the behavior and more about the pure intent to elevate the other. That is why the previous examples seem to be contradictory and yet are not.

Viktor Frankl, in *Man's Search for Meaning*, reaches this conclusion about love: "**Love is the only way to grasp another human being in the innermost core of his personality. No one can become fully aware of the very essence of another human being unless he loves him.** By his love he is enabled to see the essential traits and features in the beloved person; and even more, he sees that which is potential in him, which is not yet actualized but yet ought to be actualized. Furthermore, by his love, the loving person enables the beloved person to actualize these potentialities. By making him aware of what he can be and of what he should become, he makes these potentialities come true.... For the first time in my life I saw the truth as it is set into song by so many poets, proclaimed as the final wisdom by so many thinkers. The truth—that **Love is the ultimate and highest goal to which man can aspire.** Then I grasped the meaning of the greatest secret that human poetry and human thought and belief have to impart: **The salvation of man is through love and in love.**"

May we all look upon love more fully, more willingly. May we recognize within it the great gift that it is for us and for others. May we embrace, believe in it, and utilize it not just as the natural outcome of love the feeling (which comes and goes), but as our commitment to extend ourselves to elevate others and ourselves. Love ya!

LIFE HACK #52
THE WAY YOU PRACTICE IS THE WAY YOU PERFORM.

Chapter 53
Soulmates, MFEO's & Other Strange Things

Ready for me to burst another bubble? There is no such things as a soulmates or MFEO (made for each other). "Seriously Iuri, I'm out! I'm done with you!" "Good riddance," I say. Okay, just joking—but seriously, soulmates don't exist, at least not outside of fantasy books and inappropriate novels and novelas. **Feelings of affection and love are immensely powerful. They are life changing! I hope that you have the opportunity to fall in love, and to be loved by someone. It really is the greatest of gifts.** But what if you fall in love with Billy, and perhaps Billy falls in love with you, and because of this amazing energy that the both of you possess you begin to believe that you are soulmates, MFEO's, and you just know that there can't be anyone else besides Billy...and then he breaks up with you? Now what? If you were MFEO's...soulmates, what does this leave you with now? Nothing but hopelessness and helplessness. Now you've got to go and plead for Billy to come back, and you're going to obsess about him, and spy on him through social media to see if he's kissing anyone else. Lastly, you'll fantasize about him coming back, riding in on some white stallion. **Sista! Brotha! I love ya, but it's time to allow someone else the freedom of going elsewhere, and for you to come to realization that love will find you again,** "But Iuri, it won't be the same! I can't love anyone else like I loved Billy!" Yes, I agree with you there. **We love people uniquely. We love them for different reasons. Some more intensely, some more deeply, some more gently.** But do I have any doubt in my mind that you will love immensely again? Not at all. Live on, my friend, live on!

Really, I just want you to live realistically and in a hopeful manner. I want you to survive life's twists and turns. **I want you to rise after you fall**, with a clear understanding that the pain will pass and that God will offer other opportunities. Much love to you, my wise friend.

LIFE HACK #53
"EVERY WALL IS A DOOR."
-Ralph Waldo Emerson

Chapter 54
Closed Doors, Dark Rooms & Parked Cars

I'm so proud that you are back! I know these are awkward things to talk about, and I'm just thankful for your willingness to hear me out. **Our relationships pack a lot of punch in our lives.** I just want to offer some suggestions to ensure that they are absolutely awesome for you and don't turn into something that you look upon with regret, guilt, and shame. Can I just share my straight-up ideas with you? **We are made to connect.** The natural attraction that we have between each other, and the desire that we have to be loved, understood, and accepted, resides deeply inside of us. This often leads us to take things too far and too quickly sexually. I often explain that we use sexuality as a shortcut to feeling intimate, connected, and in a relationship.

There are no shortcuts to a healthy relationship. In my humble opinion, sexual relationships are only to occur during marriage. This last act of vulnerability—this last offering of ourselves—should only be given to those who are mature enough and committed to hold it in the highest regard, and as the ultimate union of man and woman. Treat it as holy and with an appropriate measure of respect and care. Don't abuse it; don't give it up; don't get manipulated into it; don't get guilted into it; don't do it to prove something to yourself or others; don't do it to fill your insecurities; don't do it because others are doing it or pressuring you to do it; don't do it because popular culture suggests that it's sexually mature to do so. My dear friend, don't be the one to instigate it, and don't be the one to allow it to happen.

Closed doors, dark rooms, and parked cars all make it very difficult for you to make what is by far the wisest choice for you. Remember that connection is natural, and that our bodies very much seek for comfort and pleasure. It is with that knowledge that I suggest that you **stay away from these places that will make it increasingly difficult for you to make the kind of mind-full and intelligent choices that will promote your character, reputation, and joy.** I'm serious—we are not invincible. Under intense outside and inside pressure, our wisdom, intelligence, and mind-fullness can become mind-lessness, and our actions counterproductive.

Listen to what I'm about to tell you. **When you are spending time with the opposite sex, this is a time to be mind-full, conscious, and with your eyes wide open. Do not under any circumstances engage in drinking, using drugs, or anything that alters your consciousness. Remember that the goal of the enlightened individual is mind-fullness and an increased awareness, not mind-lessness and increased ignorance.** Such a high percentage of sexual assaults, unwanted pregnancies, and other circumstances that lead to guilt and shame are accompanied by alcohol and/or other drugs. Just listen to your friend Iuri, and save yourself a world of hurt. I promise, you are not missing anything. So stay out in the light, keep your door open, and get yourself out of the car and go for a walk or a hike. Be mind-full. Be direct. Be clear.

LIFE HACK #54
THE EYES ARE USELESS, WHEN THE MIND IS BLIND.

Chapter 55
For Girls' Eyes Only

First of all, I think girls are just the most phenomenal creatures! I love your playfulness, your laughter, and your nurturing nature. I love your sense of responsibility, your pursuit of beauty, and your ability to love hard. **It's not your job to save men from themselves, but great women have been making men conscious and aware for thousands of years.** Girls, your impact on this world cannot be measured. What you will ultimately contribute as a friend, as a girlfriend, as a wife, and as a mother is remarkable. **The world is at your fingertips! Pursue great things, especially those that are of greatest value.** Do not settle for mediocrity! Do not spend time in the mundane! Do not, not ever, engage in conversation that berates or diminishes another woman or man. **Be incredibly brave, and be fierce enough to stand for decency, kindness, and truth.**

Now, there are some areas that I feel that women struggle with and, with your permission, fully acknowledging that I've never been a teenage girl, I would like to throw some suggestions your way with the hope that you'll see the logic and reason behind them. Here are some Do's and Don'ts:

- **Do not stay in any relationship that is abusive:** If a boy yells at you, hits you, pushes you, forces you to do sexual things, asks for nude pictures of you, guilts you into staying with you, threatens suicide or self-harm if you break-up with him, he is not for you. Break up, move on, and let this boy grow up and mature. No if's, and's, or but's. Don't wait for him to change, don't tell yourself that he can and will change; be done with it, and let the boy do the changing on his own— no exceptions!

- **Do not be mean to girls!** These are your sistas, your pals, your own kind. I repeatedly hear girls complain that "girls are so mean!" What the...?! How is this possible? Do not engage in gossiping about others; stop any form of backbiting; don't post negative things about one another on media; do not reject or push away other women. Instead, stand together! **A band of women is a powerful sight, and you all need each other. I think sometimes girls get competitive with each other and begin comparing themselves. This leads to feelings of jealousy, anger, insecurity, and low confidence.** Quit it, quit it, quit it. Do not compare. Remember that the good that happens to others does not mean that there is something wrong with you. Celebrate for others. Don't be petty! What are you being competitive about? Boys? Seriously? **Nothing is more unattractive to boys than an insecure girl who is mean to other girls.**

- **Stop comparing!** This is a must. Maybe there is something in you that is causing you to engage in this toxic thinking habit. I'm not opposed to looking at others and being inspired by what they are doing, but if you notice that you're comparing yourself to others and feeling worse as a result, then you can know with certainty that your comparing is out of control. Look, here's the deal—you're going to find some extraordinary people out there who appear to have it going on, and probably they do, but there's room for you, too! **There's room in this world for your brand of crazy and cool. Don't sit in the corner; don't hide in your room; don't shrink; instead, rise and become engaged in something that will expand and teach you to grow.** Here's what you do! Don't compare; admire and learn. Don't compare; instead, if you want something, make a simple plan and go get it. Don't fall into a pity party or victim mindset. Don't compare; compliment instead. Don't compare; get inspired. Don't compare; learn to admire others' strengths and ask for help in areas they are strong in and you need work on.

- **Work on your insecurities:** I find that girls often struggle with being insecure. As a result, they can become very self-critical, take things that people say personally and, as a result, struggle with anxiety and depression. **They spend too much time trying to look beautiful, instead of being beautiful in character and attitude. Perfectionism is something that seems to haunt girls especially.** They have to look this way, weigh this much, wear these clothes, talk this way, have this phone, be a part these groups, have these grades—all the while being photogenic so they can post it on Instagram. **Don't seek for perfection, seek for excellence. Don't seek to be valued by others, seek to be valuable.** Don't obsess about weight, get to work being healthy and start exercising. Don't personalize everything that people tell you and take offense—why would you do that? Consider what people say, and make intelligent decisions about what would be the very best for you...period!

- **Stay on the moral high ground. Do not sell your birthright for a mess of pottage. In other words, don't give up those things which are most precious for those of little or no value.** Do not fall for any manipulation that encourages you to go against your highest values, or to let go of those things that are most intelligent. When you make mistakes (and you will), make reparations quickly, forgive others, forgive yourself, and give yourself permission to grow from those errors.

- **Don't be drama lamas:** Sometimes drama surrounds girls. Have you ever wondered why? Perhaps it makes you feel alive, or part of something exciting. Perhaps the intensity of drama keeps you coming back for more. Don't worry, you're not the only one—millions of people watch the news and read the gossip column to get their drama fix on a daily basis. **Here's my thought for you: get busy inviting and promoting what you want out of your life, instead of critiquing other people's efforts. Stop**

adding drama to your life and the lives of others. Some girls say they're sick of the drama but are quick to put on their rubber boots and go splash around in it. It's up to you what you do. **Don't let drama be your fix for exciting, fun, and connecting to others. Find a different way to do exciting. Connect to your girls in fun, creative, and positive ways.** Stop teaching your brain to drift toward drama! Instead, teach it to move toward new skills and trusting relationships built on fun, not backbiting. **Don't sow misery, only to reap the storm. Sow appreciation, gratitude, and goodness, and you'll gain the beauty of this life.**

Girls, I love you and admire you. I'm in awe of your goodness. Your courage and awesomeness inspire me. Your ability to love is worthy of emulation. You've changed my life; now get out there and change the world!

LIFE HACK #55
"IF ALL YOU CAN DO IS CRAWL, START CRAWLING."
-RUMI

Chapter 56
For Boys' Eyes Only

Boys, buckle up—we're going for a ride. I have a lot to say to you, and to be truthful, I worry about you the very most. I've seen too many women and children who have suffered at the hands of men's ridiculous behavior. I want more for you and, to be honest, you can do and be much more. I'm discouraged about the way men are portrayed in movies and the media. Think about it for a moment. Men are presented as irresponsible, hypersexual (all they want is sex), out of control, drunkards, unable to manage emotions, idiots, with nothing inspiring to say. What the flip?! Why are men portrayed like monkeys? It drives me absolutely crazy, and you know what? It's taking a toll on us, but we are about to charge the field and rewrite our story. **It's time to be men of influence. It's time to shape the world and fight for honor, beauty, and courage. It's time to go to war against stupidity and mediocrity. Your future wife needs a warrior. Your future children need a hero. I need you to rise up and quit shrinking in the corner. I need you to get out from behind your screens and video games and engage with friends, siblings, and parents. I need you to build, create, learn, expand, have outrageous fun, make unbelievable memories. Go have an adventure that's real, and bring laughter and joy to this world.**

Here's the truth, and you need to know it. **We are warriors! We always have been. We are the builders of nations! We are protectors, influencers, and leaders.** We can't be on the sidelines...in fact, we won't be sidelined! You must not shirk the fight and retreat to your room in laziness, entranced by worthless things. **We are poets, inventors, creators.** We must not be beat down by the world. We cannot be devalued. **We must be what we can be!** Here are some do's and don'ts:

- **Pursue higher learning:** There's a trend going on, and it's been happening for a few years now, where young men aren't going to college or pursuing higher education. I've met with these young people. They are concerned about having school loans. They're worried about having a job after college. Maybe their high school experience hasn't been great, and so now they're not sure college is for them. I constantly tell people, **I would have paid triple the amount of school loans, to experience the confidence, opportunity, freedom, and income that my education has given me**. Trade schools can be extremely useful as well. Whichever one you choose, I need you to go into it with a growth mindset. You will face difficult times and struggles. This is not failure—it is the call to ask for help or to change your approach. You may fail tests and even classes. Learn to move on and grow from these experiences, understanding clearly that all of these things will give you experience and be for your good. If you're not good at something, don't worry— this is not a permanent condition. With a little bit of patience, organization, help, and effort, hard things can become easy, even enjoyable. **Begin your pursuit of education by accepting and no longer resisting the idea that learning is what you are here to do. You are either growing or dying. Flourishing or wilting. Flowing or becoming stagnant. My friend, there is no joy in wilting.** You will find no peace in stagnancy, only misery and dissatisfaction. **Choose joy and intentionally pursue the best books, education, skills, wholesome fun, awesome relationships, and spiritual wisdom.** As you do, you will find that success will follow you all of your life.

- **Treat girls and women with the utmost respect:** Listen to me, my young friend, women are absolutely remarkable. There is a tenderness in women that we would do well to learn. **Begin at home by treating your mother and sisters in the most excellent way you can manage, and then do likewise for other women and**

girls. Support them, defend them, and compliment them daily. When you are of age, date them. Don't miss a dance, and look for opportunities to spend time in the presence of these amazing creatures. Do not play them! Do not manipulate them! Never, ever, ask them for nude pictures or disrespect their bodies by touching them inappropriately, or by guilting them into doing sexual things. Do not pressure girls to have sex. I dare you and challenge you to adopt the idea that sex is much more than just something we do with our bodies. Making love is a way of making a relationship holy and the final step for those who have chosen the eternal commitment of marriage. Do not allow pornography to become a part of your personal culture. **We do not look at pornography or revealing pictures because we respect women. If they are disrobed, it is a sign of respect for their awesomeness that we look away. Please give women their privacy, and don't turn women into sexual objects. Please don't make life harder for them. Don't ogle them when they walk into the room; instead, look at their faces, smile at them, and say hello. Be that man! Be the kind of man that women feel safe and free around.**

- **Don't take yourself too seriously:** Sometimes boys can be arrogant. They think they are the cat's meow. They walk around like roosters, glaring and strutting their stuff. Do not be the ME monster where everything is about you, and you can't see other people's needs. Come on man, take it easy! Let me tell you, **there's nothing less attractive to a woman than an arrogant man. The cure for arrogance is humility and gratitude.** When people compliment you, graciously say thank you, and return a compliment. Instead of walking around in all of your state—unreachable, untouchable—be approachable and a friendly peacemaker. **Be a giver in this world, not a taker.** When you succeed at something, be grateful and help others succeed. At home, serve your mom and dad. Listen to them and ask for their advice on things. Be an awesome example to your siblings.

Humility is the mark of the enlightened individual, and thankfulness the precursor to happiness.

- **Become a peaceful warrior:** Dogs are perfect at this. They receive people with excitement and joy. They're fiercely loyal and fun. They're also great warriors and will fight to the death if the cause is great enough. **Become a dog!** Become a peacemaker in your home. **When you see your parents go greet them with a kiss, a hug, or a high-five. Ask them questions. Offer to help. Be fiercely loyal to your brothers and sisters. Hang out with them. Invite them to things with you. Your influence is enormous—it is life-changing.** Don't go around starting fires. Quit being hard-headed and hard-hearted. **A soft and willing heart is what will earn you the respect and admiration of others. It is what will bring you true success in this life.** A peaceful warrior stands up for others. He does not bully, degrade, or engage in lame gossip. He builds, not destroys. He lifts, not debases. A peaceful warrior is the greatest, because he is the servant of all. Now go to war, you peaceful warrior.

- **Become a rich man: Do not become one-dimensional; instead, become engaged in a variety of experiences, skills, and talents. Choose activities that you're naturally good at, and then engage in others that are more difficult for you.** Your future self will thank you, and so will your future wife and children...I promise! Invest in sports, arts, clubs, music, religious groups, and service opportunities. Say YES to these opportunities. Don't say lame and short sighted things like "I'm just not good at this," or "I'm just not a runner, or an artist, or a student." **Realize, this instant, that your soul can only be happy when it is expanding and growing.** Remember that your brain and body will learn whatever you repeatedly and consistently ask them to learn. So if you're not good at something, simply give it a bit of time, practice it, and experience it a bit longer, and watch it blossom inside of you. **Fill your life with wonderful things and skills, and watch your fulfilment and depth grow.** My friend, take advantage of the opportunities that are before you—no more excuses!

My dear brother and sister, I'm with you. I'm cheering for you. It doesn't matter what you've done, or haven't done, **it just takes a moment to do something great...seize that moment. Life is made up of these small moments, and an awesome life is made up of lots of little awesome events and deeds that fill those moments.** Be good, be spiritual, be kind, be outrageous! **Be an asset in your home, not a liability.** Give without expectation of return. **Pace yourself and remember to run your own race. Keep your eyes on what you can do, and when the time is right, do it!** Take care of your mistakes—your life will be full of them, and that's okay. Do not let shame fill your life. Don't hide in the dark and in secret with your mistakes—they'll poison you, I promise. Carefully select someone who can help you, and let's get you back on the glory road. Best of luck, my friend.

Life Hack #56
"Insanity is doing the same thing, over and over again, and expecting different results."
-Albert Einstein

Chapter 57
The Art of Friendship

I honestly cannot think of something that carried more importance, more happiness, more laughter, than my friendships throughout my teenage and young adult years. I believe **good friends were the difference between thinking of that time as "the best years of my life" and "the worst years of my life."** I hope you have good friends. If you don't, then let's hang out the "welcome" sign and go get some, shall we?

Friendship is an art because we are dealing with emotional creatures, not robotic ones. Friendship is about feeling trusted and giving trust. It's more about the feeling behind the words than the words themselves. It's about feeling safe, loved, and trusted by someone. You can do this! Maybe you don't think you are very good at making and keeping friends, but seriously, don't fret—there are skills you can practice that will make all the difference in the world. I'm about to throw down some knowledge about how to make and keep friends, so listen up:

- **Hang out the "all are welcome" sign:** Don't leave your house like a peacock, wearing a sign that screams, "I'm too cool for you," "I'm unapproachable," "I'm pissed off," "I'm afraid of people," "It's all about me," or "I'm so into my music that I don't want to talk to anyone." Seriously, **what sign do you wear when you leave your home, when you walk down the halls of your school, when you are sitting down in class, when you are at lunch?** If you are wearing any of these signs, it's time to take them off and put out the "all are welcome" sign. Here are some other signs you can wear:

  - "I'm a loyal friend."

  - "I like people."

- "Wanna have some fun?"

- "I'm a great listener."

- "Got friends? I'll be yours."

- "You can talk to me."

- "I'm happy to see you."

- "You make my day."

- "I got your back."

- **Just smile and wave:** A great way to hang out the "welcome" sign is by simply smiling at people. You don't have to freak people out by throwin' out a creepy smile—a gentle one will do. Here's how you do it: make eye contact, throw down a gentle smile, wave, call people by name, and say hello.

- **Remember people's names:** It's been said that a person's name is more important than all of the other names in the world combined. **People like to hear their name. They like to be recognized and remembered.** So when you meet people and they tell you their name, immediately inside your head repeat their name three times in a phrase, and then use their name right away.

- **Don't gossip about or criticize others:** Do not gossip, because the only message that you are sending out to others is, "When you're not around, I'm going to talk badly about you." Not a great message! In fact, I want you to start something new: **practice the art of positive gossip! Make it a point to speak positively of others. Compliment others around other people.** Is it inspiring? Is it nice? Is it helpful? Is it kind? If the answer is yes, then it has passed the test, and you should say it. Don't criticize others, either. **Being critical of others just provokes defensiveness and lets them know that you're not a safe friend.** Stay away from it.

- **Become excited when you see your friends:** Dogs are amazing at this skill. Think about it. They bark, jump, wag their tails, wet themselves, run around in circles, smile (right?). Everything about their behavior says, "I am happy to see you!" Don't wag your bum, wet yourself, or run around in circles—you'll just look crazy...actually, go for it! **Raise your arms, smile, hug, high-five, call out their name, do a cool handshake or something else amazing when you see your friends coming toward you.**

- **Be interested in your friends:** This is key! **Be interested in what they do, what they think, what they like.** Ask them about their lives and then be a great listener. You'll make and keep more friends by simply paying attention to what they are telling you, showing more interest, and by asking additional questions. **Remember, if you want people to like you...like them.**

- **Be a loyal friend:** Stand by your people. **When they succeed, be happy with them. When tragedy strikes, sorrow with them.** Make time for them in your life. Invite them to come to your home, take them out to lunch, go to a movie, do homework together, go to a concert or event together, go on a road trip, have an adventure together, or exercise together. **Remember their birthdays and make a big deal about them.** In sum, **be a great friend, and you'll likely have great friends.**

- **When it doesn't work, go again—and again:** Look, the reality is that some people just will not want to be your friends. That's the deal! You'll do all the right stuff, but they're just not interested. Expect it, so that when it happens you can say, "Oh yeah, Iuri said this would happen. This kind of hurts, but I must move on and keep trying because this just matters too much." Like I've told you before, sometimes people will choose you, other times they won't. I bet if you take a close look at yourself, you'll realize that this is true for you as well. **Make a list of 5 to 10 people that you** would like to have as friends, and then begin to use these skills to see if you can land a good one.

- **Be at the right place, at the right time, with the right people:** Quit hiding in your room or behind a screen for heaven's sake! **Listen to me—get engaged and get involved NOW! Put yourself around people consistently, doing similar things, and you'll find that friendships naturally will flourish.** Here are some ways you can do this:

  - Join a team or sport (you know I don't care if you are good at it, just do it!).
  - Become a member of a club.
  - Join a church or religious group.
  - Attend games, activities, and dances.
  - Join choir, orchestra, theater plays, student groups, associations, etc.
  - Get a job.

Okay, no more excuses. No more, "friends are just too much work," or "I don't want to be part of the drama," or "I don't need friends"—bruh, you need them and want them. Let's move beyond the past hurt and failures and move courageously toward friendship. I got your back! Make that list of people you can start focusing your efforts on, and let's get to it. I wish you the very best.

LIFE HACK #57

"YOU ARE NOT A DROP IN THE OCEAN.
YOU ARE THE ENTIRE OCEAN IN A DROP."
-RUMI

CHAPTER 58
BIRDS OF A FEATHER

Hey there, I hope you're enjoying the book so far. I want to keep chatting about friends a bit more. The people we invest our time and energy with just matter so very much. You've probably noticed at your school that people have a tendency to stick together in little pods, groups, or cliques. This is normal. I know we usually talk about it in negative ways, such as, "My school is too cliquey," but I don't think we need to make a big deal about this. **I think it's natural for people to stick around others who have similar interests and who think in similar ways. Don't let this be a deterrent that keeps you stuck and bitter.** The problem is that sometimes these groups or cliques become exclusive and condemning of others. The key here is to **be inclusive and to expand beyond your own circle**. If you find yourself in a gathering of people, use the confidence that comes from numbers to reach out to others and include them. **Brotha or sista, there is so much good that you can do! I'm telling you, the simple gesture of inviting someone to your table, walking with them down the hall, or sitting by them in a bus can be a game changer.**

If you find yourself on the outside and disconnected, don't fret too much, but it's time to put a plan into action. Here's the great news for you: **90% of the people in your school are looking for a great friend!** Sometimes we fool ourselves into thinking that everyone is already spoken for, and that we are the only ones lacking—this isn't true! **Switch your mindset from "Everyone is taken," to "Everyone is looking for a friend."**

Here's my other thought about friends and groups. You may find yourself in a group that is experimenting with drugs, sex, stealing, fighting, etc. **Let me be honest—this is not wise. Remember that our goal is to be wise and to make intelligent choices.**

Choices that will enhance our future and expand our choices, not shrink our future opportunity. Don't get sucked into things that will take away your opportunities and freedom in life. **I think the pull of connection, and wanting to be liked, loved, and valued sometimes keeps us in relationships and groups that kill our future, keep us angry, and create all sorts of conflict in our lives. My friend, don't do this to yourself. Do not dig potholes in your present and future.** I know that it's amazing to feel included, but if you are feeling at home in a group that does things like that, it's time for your logic and reason to take over, and for you to think over some things. **We're talking common sense, not rocket science!** You must not lie to yourself and pretend that you're only going to do this for a while. You can't pretend to be a victim and lie to yourself that this is the only place that will accept you. **Don't be a martyr and blame others for the choices you're making.** I plead with you—there are greener pastures and more encouraging people. I realize that this may take a significant amount of willpower and support. Shifting cultures requires courage and grit. **It may take people around you time to see how amazing you are. It may take you some time to see how amazing they are—time is your friend.**

Birds of a feather have a tendency to flock together. But you are a different bird now. Have lots of friends from lots of cliques with different interests. Don't get caught up in hateful and exclusive groups. Expand your horizons. Enhance your vision, and become loyal to wisdom, to the best ideas, and to individuals.

LIFE HACK #58

"THAT WHICH WE PERSIST IN DOING BECOMES EASIER FOR US TO DO—NOT THAT THE NATURE OF THE THING IS CHANGED, BUT THAT OUR POWER TO DO IS INCREASED."

-HEBER J. GRANT (PARAPHRASING RALPH WALDO EMERSON)

Chapter 59
Let your Parents Parent

I hope you have good parents. I hope they love you and treat you with kindness. I hope they are loyal to you and are exemplary in their actions. **Parents have a lot to give. Their experience matters. What they've seen and gone through is of great importance, even if it happened a thousand years ago (yeah, we're that old).** But as you probably know and may have even experienced, we are not perfect. In fact, we are way below perfect. When dealing with your parents, do so with patience. Your opinions matter; your ideas are important; but what they think matters as well. Let me show you something. I find that parents and adolescents often disagree over these things:

Parents want...	You want...
Safety	Fun
Responsibility	Freedom
More engagement with family	More time with friends
Open communication	Privacy
You to think about your future	To think about now
You to respect them	Them to respect you
You to meet their expectations	To do what you want to do
Discipline	Parents to accept what you're doing

Here's the secret: you're both right. Yes, I want the party, the cake, and to eat it too! I want to have what is on both sides. **The problem is that when parents and teens argue, they often become stuck defending their side and forget that real success will**

come from learning to negotiate and think in a win-win kind of way. It's possible, I promise.

Look, I don't have your parents here in front of me—I can't tell them what to do. But you are here, and you and I can be reasonable and begin to change how things flow in your home. Seeing where your parents are coming from can help you stay calm, and not turn into a rabid animal. Louis Pasteur said that "chance favors the prepared mind." When you understand and prepare for what's coming, you can be more patient, and when you are more patient and mind-full, better outcomes follow. Here is the best part: if you are able to come to table reasonably and let your parents parent you a little bit, you'll actually get more of what you want. In other words, **doing more of what they desire means you'll get to do more of what you desire**—brilliant, huh?

Remember that you are powerful. You can walk into a room and influence the mood of that room. When you are respectful, kind, and willing to listen, you inspire your parents to do the same. When you are unreasonable, disrespectful, and uncompromising, you'll invite the same behavior from your parents. What's our goal? It is to be intelligent and to allow wisdom to rule our actions. When that happens we all win. Learn to speak their language a bit. **Use open communication to soothe their concerns and to help them build trust in you. Tell them you're wanting to have a lot of fun, but that you will be reasonable and be safe. When you come home from school, don't run and hide in your room; go find your mom and dad and tell them about your day. Spend time with your family willingly and without complaining. Speak to them in a respectful manner and, as you do, you'll find that their level of trust in you increases, and then you won't have to sneak around to do what you want.** Git 'er done!

Life Hack #59

"Everyone has a plan until they get punched in the face."

-Mike Tyson

Chapter 60
The Art of War

Your life is full of critical conversations—conversations that will arouse emotions of anger, frustration, defensiveness, fear, and sadness inside of you. These emotions are hard to handle and, as a result, they often overwhelm the mind and body, turning us into primates. When this happens, we end up yelling at each other, we become defensive, closed down, and not a lot of progress occurs. Listen to what I'm about to tell you: **Conflict is essential in life, and a significant part of your happiness depends upon your ability to navigate it masterfully. Yes, you must become a Jedi Master when handling conflict.** Why? Because I want you to turn your arguments into moments of opportunity and growth. Sometimes things build up, or we end up stuck in a rut; effective discussions can unblock these problems and propel us toward better times. Here are 10 amazing tips for you to remember when you are having a difficult conversation with someone at home, work, or school:

1. **Talk less, listen more:** Listen to the words that people say. We often get stuck in the emotion, or the tone, or the body language, but the key is to listen to the words that are being spoken, and ask whether they carry value for you. Listen, don't interrupt. Hear people, don't talk over them.

2. **Stay humble:** If you can do this during an argument, you will be a true Jedi Master, and your arguments will become a true source of victory. Be willing to listen to what is being argued, and consider it deeply. If it is useful information, use it, and you'll be better for it. If after consideration you decide it is not the best course of action, then express gratitude, and respectfully disagree.

3. **Watch your language:** Your words are potent and can be the difference between a successful discussion and a disaster. Remember that words are tools. If you use them accurately and wisely, good outcomes are more likely to result. If you start flinging words around like hammers in a china shop, things get ugly real quick...right? Follow these tips to become amazing:

    a. **Don't use generalizations:** Quit using phrases like "You never listen," or "You always yell at me," or "It's never what I want." These generalization are inaccurate, and as such should not be part of your vocabulary. Remove them from your arguments.

    b. **Don't swear at each other:** Words can be explosive. Unless you are trying to provoke an argument or pick a fight, profanity is not effective in arguments. Use soft and respectful language to invite a better outcome.

4. **Work the problem:** This is essential. When people argue they often forget the problem and begin attacking each other. This is called criticism. The difference sounds like this: "This is a problem, let's fix it," versus, "You're the problem, let's fix you." One inspires solutions, the other provokes war and defensiveness. Work hard to keep your focus, so you don't get caught up and tripped up in your and other's emotions. Stay focused on the problem so that you can resolve it, and work out some solutions—instead of attacking the individual.

5. **Don't dig up the past:** Man, we are infamous at this blunder. This is a common way that people get themselves in trouble during conflict. Work the problem that is happening right now—don't bring up the junk from the past.

6. **Don't use machine gun tactics:** This refers to when people bring up a slew of issues from the past and just ambush you with them, all at once. This could be things you've said, or what you meant, or things that you did. This tactic is good for overwhelming someone, and leaving them

bewildered and bleeding all over the ground, but if this is not your intention, then try sticking to the issue at hand. Work the problem, right?

7. **Don't shut down:** Often when we feel that we can't win an argument, or when someone says something that is offensive, we go into shutdown mode. Remember, you don't have to run! You can handle difficult emotions and hard conversations! Keep your eyes and ears open. Pay attention, and respond in a mind-full (aware, deliberate, and congruent) way.

8. **Don't turn into a mind-reader:** Remember that we are terrible at mind-reading. Don't assume you know what the other person is thinking or what their intent is. If you think something is happening, ask a question—don't assume!

9. **Improve in these areas:** Use these words as guides for how you should conduct relationships and disagreements:

   a. Patience: Hang in there. Don't fight, flee, or freeze. Focus on using this event as an opportunity.

   b. Long-suffering: Sounds like a tough one, right? Your ability to withstand difficult emotions while staying focused and mind-full is a beautiful thing. Develop some emotional muscles.

   c. Kindness: Soft words yield a softer outcome.

   d. Gentleness: A soft answer turns away wrath. Remember to invite and promote the outcome you want. Gentle invites gentle...try it!

   e. Humility: Staying curious and open during an argument is essential. If you are closed, stubborn, and arrogant, that will only produce more fighting and more resistance in the other person.

   f. No manipulation: Don't threaten, manipulate, or use emotional blackmail. Stay flexible and avoid punishing the other person with words, deeds, or silence.

g. Repair quickly: When feelings are hurt and relationships battered by an argument, go make amends, and let the individual know that you love them, and that you'll do a bit better next time. Be brave and consistent with this step.

10. **Don't start an argument in the first place:** Remember to start conversations softly and respectfully. This will keep conversations going smoothly, and you'll avoid the minefield that conflict can become.

My friend, learn these well, and become a relationship master, instead of a relationship disaster. Don't automatically see things as attacks. See them differently, and you'll act differently. Best of luck to you.

LIFE HACK #60

"IT IS BETTER TO BE THOUGHT A FOOL, THAN TO OPEN ONE'S MOUTH
AND REMOVE ALL DOUBT."
-MARK TWAIN

CHAPTER 61
ASK FOR HELP

Are you the kind of person that asks for help? Are you secure enough in yourself to do so? I visit with so many youth who struggle with heartache, high levels of stress, and the discouraging feelings that follow failure. I meet youth who have fallen behind in school to the point that they don't want to go to class anymore because they are so lost in there. I know this feeling well because I've been there. **Something happens when we fail repeatedly at something—we get angry at it and we turn against it.** Here's how it happened to me. Notice how I became poisoned—and poisonous. I was taking a math class and I started to not understand the material. I didn't ask for help so I began to fail the tests and stopped doing the homework. Going to class was embarrassing because I didn't understand the material. I started hating math. I would avoid it. I spoke badly about it. I hated the teacher. I started saying, "Math is useless. I'll never use this stuff for the rest of my life!" The outcome? Yeah, I failed the dang thing, and felt even worse. **Math was not the problem...I was the problem**. **It wasn't math I had a problem with—it was failing I hated, and that embarrassment and anger corrupted my insides.** I needed help, because I seriously did not understand it, but unfortunately I didn't ask for it; instead, I became angry, bitter, and reaped even more failure.

We don't just follow this destructive little pattern with math—we do it with other things as well. We do it with activities that are hard for us or that we fail at, and we even do it within our own families. Perhaps your parents are critical. Maybe they fight with you. Perhaps you feel that they are nicer to your other siblings, and you feel they are not being fair (remember the F-word?) with you. You begin to feel like the scapegoat or the black sheep in your home. This is dangerous ground, because if you are not watchful, the pattern I described above will begin to develop here. Here's what it might look like: You begin to feel like you can't do anything right with your family. You start to avoid them by going to your room, not talking to them, avoiding family activities, and not coming home. You begin to dislike your family (maybe even hate them). You speak badly about them. You treat your parents and siblings badly. Things become even worse. You don't like coming home. You start dreaming about leaving as soon as you turn 18. The outcome is more hurt, more anger, and more disconnect. It's a tragedy of enormous proportions. **Do not, I repeat, do NOT allow this corrupting pattern to develop within you. Do not draw away from the things that matter most to those that are of no worth, simply because you are mad.**

I've watched this happen to church-going individuals as well. They begin to make some mistakes in the way they live. They feel guilty. They feel judged by church-goers. They begin to dislike church people. They avoid going to church and activities related to church. They begin to hate church, and speak badly about it and the people in it. They determine that church isn't for them, and fight with their parents about going. They leave the church.

So much of this can be avoided if we just **adopt the mindset of asking for help when things become too difficult or when we make mistakes.** You can avoid tragedy by simply asking, "Can you help me? I need a little help here." The words are simple, they are true, and they can save you from that poisonous pattern described above. If you are falling behind, just ask for help from a teacher, a school counselor, or your parents, and get a tutor already! If you are fighting at home, ask for help from your friends (instead of complaining to them), talk to your parents and ask for their help, see a therapist, talk to a school counselor or a religious leader that can help.

Don't allow pride, embarrassment, and stubbornness to harden your heart. Why not stay soft-hearted? Why not admit that you need help? Why not remain humble and teachable? It's normal to fail. It's expected that you won't understand everything. It's possible that you won't know how to handle every situation. Is this not reasonable? Of

course it is! Asking for help is a sign of intelligence, not weakness.

My friend, don't allow your mistakes, failures, and challenges to turn into anger. If you are not good at something right now, remember that your body and brain will learn anything you consistently teach them. It may just take a little time. You may need a tutor. **Develop a little endurance, for heaven's sake! Keep your life open. Don't close doors and turn your back on things because they are not turning out the way you want them right now. Use your highest reasoning abilities to decide what you will keep and pursue, and what you won't. How intelligent is it to turn your back on things that are good for your body, mind, and spirit?** Don't use "this is just too hard" (waah, waah, waah), or "I'm just not good at it" as your measuring scale for what you will pursue and what you won't pursue. Instead, use this:

- Is it physically healthy? Then do it.
- Is it spiritually healthy? Stick with it.
- Is it intelligent? Go for it.
- Is it wise? That's your ticket.
- Is is social? Be brave, take a risk, and be vulnerable.
- Is it a skill that will bring you joy in the future? Get your rear in gear and get to it.
- Will it make you more employable? Move in that direction.
- Will it make your future brighter and give you more opportunity? Take that road.

Don't quit on school! Don't quit on your family! Don't quit on your friends! Don't let your momentary struggles, mistakes, and failures become your permanent destiny. I believe in you wholeheartedly. I'm cheering for you. I can't wait to see what you'll come up with. People are amazing. You're amazing! But even you, in all of your grandeur, will need a helping hand. Ask for it, and when it's given, take it!

Life Hack #61

"Do not pray for an easy life, pray for the strength to endure a difficult one."
-Bruce Lee

Chapter 62
Invest, Invest, Invest

Your relationships are by far the most valuable commodity in your life. Keeping those relationships healthy, fun, safe, and awesome is a worthwhile investment. It's the gift that will just keep on giving and giving. Think of your relationships in terms of ratios. A good relationship will have a ratio of 5 to 1—that is, five positive interactions for each negative one. A great relationship will have a ratio of 10 to 1 or even 20 to 1. That is our goal! Your job at home, with parents, with siblings, at school, with teachers, with friends, is to keep your relationships flowing in the positive. Stephen Covey, in his landmark book *The 7 Habits of Highly Effective People*, described this simple concept by using the term "emotional bank account." Make sure that the emotional bank account between you and your parents and you and your friends is in the black (good), instead of in the red (not so good). The way we keep our emotional bank accounts happy is by making constant investments (deposits) into them (and limiting our withdrawals). Don't complicate this process—it's really quite simple. Investments can be small and simple, though over time, they will amount to beautiful things. Let me give you some examples:

- When you wake up in the morning, say good morning to your parents and siblings.
- Ask people how their sleep was and what they dreamed about.
- Listen to people and ask more questions.
- Express gratitude for food.
- When you leave for school, say goodbye to your family, give a hug or kiss, tell them you love them.

- Clean your room, make your bed, and pick up your junk off the ground.
- Offer to do dishes, take out the trash, set the table, clear the table, or fill someone's cup.
- Greet your friends with a hug, smiles, excitement, and interest.
- Say hello to people in the hall, call them by name, and high-five them.
- Say hi to your teachers. Ask them how their day is. Be nice to them.
- Text something fun and friendly to your mom, dad, siblings, or friends during the day.
- Expand your circle of friends and be friendlier to others.
- When you get home go find your parents. Greet them with a kiss, hug, or kind words.
- Ask them, "Do you need help with something today?" (They'll flip out!)
- Ask them about their day. Tell them about your day...don't spare the details.
- Compliment your siblings and ask them about their day.
- Do a little bit of service around your home.
- Text your friends and invite them to your home.
- Make a plan to do something with them outside of your home.
- Eat dinner with your family. Be grateful for the food. Help to clean up.
- Play games with your family, pray with them, have fun with them.
- Take time to tell your parents about your life. Ask them for help with something.
- Be patient with them and forgive them.

- Always say please and thank you.

- Kiss your parents good night, and tell them you love them.

Of course there are millions of examples, and unlimited ways that you can expand your efforts. Remember to K.I.S.S. it (keep it simple, stupid). Don't complicate it. **Know that by small and simple investments, great fortunes are made. A little here, a little there.** Remember your ratios. Keep them in the overwhelming positive. **It's important to note that we are always either investing or withdrawing from our emotional bank accounts. Relationships are about giving, taking, and receiving. Make sure that you are a giver of life, trust, fun, and safety in your relationships, and not a vampire.** Now get out there and SHOW ME THE MONEY!

LIFE HACK #62
"ALL GENERALIZATIONS ARE FALSE, INCLUDING THIS ONE."
-MARK TWAIN

Awesome Advice
If You're a Believer

SOME WORDS BEFORE WE GET STARTED...

I am a Christian. I believe and have come to know, with some degree of certainty, that Jesus Christ was more than a man, more than a teacher, more than a prophet. He was the promised Messiah, the Son of God, and ultimately the Savior of the world. Why does this matter? Well, it matters a lot to me, and I hope you'll soon find that it means a lot to you as well. Jesus was the most extraordinary teacher and revolutionary. **The doctrine that He unveiled to the world was simply breathtaking and perspective-enhancing. The marvelous hope and peace that come from that doctrine is a marvelous treasure; in fact, it is the most valuable *pearl of great price.***

I'm a social scientist and therapist by trade. I have now sat face-to-face, knee-to-knee, eyeball-to-eyeball with thousands of people over a fifteen-year span. I am fascinated by the way people think, why they do what they do, and the internal doctrine (ideas, beliefs, and philosophies) that drives their choices. **Psychology is everything! One's perspective and lens with which they look out at the world with is of critical importance.** Because of its dramatic relevance, this lens requires attention. It demands constant care and cleaning. For our joy, peace, and hope to be full, our personal lens has to reflect the truth of things as they were, as they are, and as they will be. **This search for truth is the great adventure of life.** Uncovering it is the great mystery that Jesus repeatedly prompts us to seek and to find; to knock and it shall be opened; to ask and it shall be given unto you. **Let me tell you—you will most certainly find whatever it is you are looking for. Choose to seek the Gospel and it will find you.**

Belief and faith are not the easiest of things. There are many competing theories of life—ideas about why we are here and where we are going. Science gives us some remarkable understanding into the things that God has orchestrated, and yet it does not speak of purpose, meaning, or of things spiritual. **Marrying your faith to science is a match made in heaven. There need be no competition.** We don't know all of the answers, and we certainly don't know how God accomplishes all of His purposes. Some things we will never know until the day we die and meet our Maker. Until then we must live by faith, with a brightness of hope, and full of charity. **In the end we must choose to believe in God. We must choose to follow Christ. We must choose the Gospel as our quest. It all comes down to choice...how simple and frightening!** But the Gospel is not something to fear—it is something to love and embrace. It is individual, meaning that you must embrace it personally, and yet the consequences of that choice will reverberate throughout your whole being, and reach everyone you come in contact with. Your choice here matters. Don't ever pretend that it doesn't.

There is knowledge everywhere. Some of it is worthless, and some of it is of great worth. **The most important knowledge that I'm continually coming to understand is this: God is my Heavenly Father. He is aware of me, and in some cosmic way, He knows me and cares for me. I am His purpose, His focus, and His glory**. His whole goal is for me to return to Him with the most valuable life experience possible. His loyalty is enduring. His trust is humbling. His love is life-giving. I believe! But belief and faith are never places of arrival. They are never destinations. These things are meant to be fed, nurtured, cared for, or they will likely wither, die, and become overrun by the weeds of this world.

My dear friends, **I urge you in the kindest of ways to seek for this Jesus of Nazareth. I invite you to seek with patience. I've long understood that the truths of this life are revealed little by little, line upon line, precept upon precept.** A sure witness or testimony is not a Google search away, nor does it often come as a flood of revelation. It is something that comes small by small and slow by slow. Stick with it! You're meant to doubt, to have questions. It's not all roses and candy, for heaven's sake. Conflict and struggle will come, and when they do, be prayerful and patiently seek your Heavenly Father, the scriptures, and those who can strengthen you. I believe in you, and in your ability to accomplish what to you may seem impossible things. "Shall we not go forward in so great a cause?" YES, we shall and we must.

Your fellow disciple in Christ,
Iuri Tiago Melo

CHAPTER 63
THE PARABLE OF THE SOWER

Christ was the ultimate teacher. He often used parables that were simple to understand as a way to help the hearer see himself more clearly, and to teach eternal principles. I've always loved the parable of the sower, or, as it is also known, the parable of the soils. I'll tell it to you in my own way:

A man went out to sow seeds. I can imagine him with a bag full of seeds, walking through the fields, throwing the seeds as he walks. Some of the seeds fell upon the many paths that criss-crossed the field. Some fell on stony ground. Some fell among weeds and thorns, and some fell on good soil. The ones that fell upon the many paths were eaten by the birds. Those that fell upon stony ground took root and grew quickly, but when the sun rose they were scorched, because they had no root. Those that fell among the weeds and thorns grew as well, but over time were choked and starved by the weeds and thorns. Those that fell upon the good soil grew and gave much fruit, some thirtyfold, some sixtyfold, some an hundredfold. As Jesus finished the parable, the apostles were confused and did not know the meaning of the parable, and sought some clarification. Jesus explained (once again in my own words):
The seeds that fell by the wayside or on the many paths signify those who hear the word of God but do not understand it nor do they believe it, and straightway are eaten up by the Adversary. Those that fell upon stony ground represent those who receive the gospel with gladness and endure for a while, but they have no root in themselves, and so when the challenges of the world come, they become offended, and the seedling is burned by the intensity of the sun. Those that fell among thorns also signify those who receive the word of God and begin to grow at first, and yet they become overwhelmed

by and concerned about the cares and the riches of the world, and ultimately become unfruitful. The seeds that fell upon good soil grow, flourish, and give forth much fruit, some an hundredfold, some sixty, some thirty, symbolic of those who receive and embrace the Gospel with open hearts and are, accordingly, richly blessed.

Master storyteller... just absolute sheer genius. For me there are three essential questions that this parable begs to have answered:

1. **So, what is this parable truly about?** This parable is really about the state of your heart. Is your heart closed, stony, and full of weeds, or is it open, soft, and broken, ready to receive the word of God? Perhaps you can see yourself in this parable. Has the word of God made its way into you to the point that it's giving forth good fruit—thirtyfold, sixtyfold, or a hundredfold? Or has it become overrun by other less important things that make you unfruitful? Does the word of God work within you, or have you become offended by the challenges, struggles, and demands of Christian discipleship? In this wonderful parable, **Jesus invites us to prepare our hearts not only to receive his word but to live the kind of life that produces wonderful, sweet, and life-giving fruit**. He invites us to have a willing heart and a contrite spirit.

2. **What is the seed?** The seed is the word of God, as found in the scriptures and spoken by those who are called of God.

3. **What is the difference between the four different kinds of soil?** The difference is that the good soil was prepared. The rocks had been removed from it. The weeds and thorns were gone and the ground was soft and broken by the plow, ready for planting.

How is your heart? I believe your heart is much like a garden. It must be tended on a daily basis to produce fruit. The weeds must be plucked; the precious plants must be protected against insects. The ground must be given nutrients for each seedling to grow and for each plant to provide its bounty. **My friend, keep your heart clean and free from things that will**

choke it and make it unfruitful, and you will receive the harvest that comes from a soft and willing heart. Remember, "By their fruits ye shall know them."

LIFE HACK #63

PRAY DELIBERATELY, NOT REPETITIVELY.

Chapter 64
Faith - Belief - Knowledge

Hello, you amazing person! Let's talk about faith and knowledge. From Paul we learn that there is substance and evidence to faith. From Alma, we learn that when we have faith, we hope for things that are not seen, but which are true. **Faith is a principle of power. It is something that moves us toward those things we desire and hope for.** A goal that you set and move toward is in part motivated by the simple faith and hope that you will accomplish it and receive the reward. We all use faith—it's natural, **but the Gospel emphasizes a special type of faith—faith in Jesus Christ. Why? Because there is power in Christ.** I can hope and have faith that a tree will heal me, but there is no power in that tree. We can believe that the universe will align things for us in our lives, but the universe is not an entity, it's just space matter. We can have faith that our horoscopes are real, and really telling us things that are true, but really, they are just words on a page and vague generalizations that apply to everyone ("Dude! What? I totally was believing those, Iuri!" Sorry to burst your bubble, my friend.).

Christ is the great mediator of all men. He stands between you and your Father in Heaven. He is the one pleading your case before God. His love and sacrifice for you have placed Him at the center of your life. His willingness to descend below all things, and to succor you in your scandal and errors, is why He is known as the great physician. He is real. His love is life-saving, and the atonement which He performed is the central act of all creation that will ultimately bring us all back to God. He did not shirk; He drank the bitter cup, and in those moments He freed us from both physical and spiritual death. He is the way, and that is why we must have faith in Him and follow Him.

224

You may hear people testify, witness, or say they know that Christ lives, or that God is real. You may wonder how they have come to know this. Perhaps you have even wondered if you will ever know for yourself. Much of that answer will depend upon your seeking, asking, and following. Christ stated, "If any man will do His will, he shall know of the doctrine, whether it be of God, or whether I speak of myself." Thus, **to truly know, you must experiment upon the word, and by and by, you will receive "evidence," and "substance" that what you have faith in, is real.**

Think of faith on a continuum or a scale, beginning at no knowledge, growing to belief, progressing to faith, and moving toward knowledge. Imagine a small seed in the ground (no knowledge). Imagine that seedling beginning to grow and breaking through the ground toward the light (belief). See the seed becoming a small tree, bearing some fruit and rooting itself to the ground (faith). Visualize this seed growing into a well established tree, bearing much fruit and establishing a deep network of roots (this is knowledge). It's important to realize that **faith is a type of knowledge. It doesn't mean zero knowledge—it implies knowledge in the state of evolution. As you feed and nurture that seed, it will grow and expand within you, ultimately maturing into a tree and a deeper assurance of the things you have faith in.**

It's also important to realize that faith and knowledge are never places of arrival—you are never done. **The Gospel is dynamic and so is life. Things are constantly on the move in your mind and, as a result, faith, belief, and knowledge must be fed constantly, or they will simply lose power and dry up. It's a basic reality of life: what you feed grows, what you neglect dies...such is life, my friend.** So as you seek to expand your faith, do so by feeding it with good information and good works.

Your testimony of God, Jesus Christ, and the Gospel are your most precious possession. Invest your time, effort, and energies here. Do so patiently. The strength of a tree and a deep network of roots is not found in a Google search—it is found as we search diligently over large

expanses of time, and as we engage the Gospel in our lives. Over time the Lord will bless you with precious moments that reveal His love for you and the truth about the things you have faith in. It is the law of the harvest, and He is pleading with you to trust Him in this testimony-building process. I'm reminded of something I read a long time ago: **"If it's true [the Gospel, and that God lives and loves us], what else matters?" Think of it—what else even competes with that knowledge?** What else competes with the understanding that you lived with God before you were born? That God has a plan of happiness for you while you are here? That Christ is the Savior of the world, and as we follow him, we can inherit all that God has...everything!? That we will live after we die, and can return to live with God again, and experience the quality of His life? As Paul said, "Eye hath not seen, nor ear heard, neither have entered into the heart of man, the things which God hath prepared for them that love him." Everything else is trivial compared to the knowledge and glory that God has in store for us. Seek and you will most certainly find. Knock, and over time it will be opened unto you. Ask, and then open your ears, your mind, and your heart so that you may receive. "He that hath ears to hear, let him hear."

LIFE HACK #64
"THE BEST WAY OUT IS ALWAYS THROUGH."
-ROBERT FROST

Chapter 65
Use it or Lose it

I love small stories that pack a big punch. The story of the soap maker and the rabbi are a good example of that. Check it out:

There once was an old soap maker who did not believe in God. One day as he was walking with a rabbi, he said, "There is something I cannot understand. We have had religion for thousands of years. But everywhere you look there is evil, corruption, dishonesty, injustice, pain, hunger, and violence. It appears that religion has not improved the world at all. So I ask you, what good is it?" The rabbi did not answer for a time, but continued walking with the soap maker. Eventually they approached a playground where children, covered in dust, were playing in the dirt. "There is something I don't understand," the rabbi said. "Look at those children. We have had soap for thousands of years, and yet those children are filthy. What good is soap?" The soap maker replied, "But rabbi, it isn't fair to blame soap for these dirty children. Soap has to be used before it can accomplish its purpose." The rabbi smiled and said, "Exactly."

The application of the Gospel in your life is by far the most intelligent choice you will make. As you apply it, the doctrines of faith, hope, and charity will make their way deeply into your bones, influence your thoughts, penetrate your feelings, and ultimately help you become something glorious.

I once traveled to Hawaii and became aware of a couple of words that capture this process well. The words are "Mana" and "Pono." *Mana* is divine power and influence. *Pono* is most often defined as righteousness, and when someone is *Pono*, it usually signifies that they are living a life of full integrity, and that all is well and right. **So if you want the *Mana*, do, or become *Pono*!**

Remember that the Gospel is about the evolution of the self, the domestication of the primitive man, and ultimately becoming more like Jesus Christ. I'm fond of C.S. Lewis's small analogy of our life as a house: *"Imagine yourself as a living house. God comes in to rebuild that house. At first, perhaps, you can understand what He is doing. He is getting the drains right and stopping the leaks in the roof and so on; you knew that those jobs needed doing and so you are not surprised. But presently He starts knocking the house about in a way that hurts abominably and does not seem to make any sense. What on earth is He up to? The explanation is that He is building quite a different house from the one you thought of—— throwing out a new wing here, putting on an extra floor there, running up towers, making courtyards. You thought you were being made into a decent little cottage: but He is building a palace. He intends to come and live in it Himself."* **This radical transformation from a yurt to a royal palace is what Christianity is all about. God intends to root out the natural creature from within us and turn us into spiritual beings. This mighty transformation requires mighty work over an extended period of time.**

Perhaps no invitation carries more bewilderment into the heart of a Christian than Jesus' admonition for us to become perfect as He is, and as God is. C.S. Lewis spoke about this very thing in his brilliant book Mere Christianity. Check it out: *"The command Be ye perfect [Matt. 5:48] is not idealistic gas. Nor is it a command to do the impossible. He is going to make us into creatures that can obey that command. He said (in the Bible) that we were "gods" and he is going to make good His words. If we let Him—for we can prevent Him, if we choose—He will make the feeblest and filthiest of us into a god or goddess, a dazzling, radiant, immortal creature, pulsating all through with such energy and joy and wisdom and love as we cannot now imagine, a bright stainless mirror which reflects back to God perfectly (though of course, on a smaller scale) His own boundless power and delight and goodness. The process will be long and in parts very painful; but that is what we are in for. Nothing less. He meant what he said"* **Remember that God's timeline for the attainment of this goal is eternity.** Earth is a stop (albeit an important one) along the way. **It's also important to realize that this is not the martyr's path; instead, it is the warrior's path. It is not all suffering and deprivation. I have come to know that path of discipleship is an immensely joyous one. It is the only path I know of that can speak confidence and hope to the most frightened parts of me.** The gospel truly is marrow to the bones, life to the heart, vision to the eyes, and peace to the mind. Remember Paul's encouraging words: "For God hath not given us the spirit of fear; but of power, and of love, and of a sound mind." To those add the encouraging invitation of the Savior to "Come unto me all ye that labour and are heavy laden, and I will give you rest."

Want the Mana? Become Pono... Aloha!

LIFE HACK #65
"GOD'S EXTRAORDINARY WORK IS MOST OFTEN DONE BY ORDINARY PEOPLE."
-NEAL A. MAXWELL

CHAPTER 66
THE LORD'S SCIENTIFIC METHOD

When I was 20 years old I spent two years serving a religious mission in New Jersey and Pennsylvania. It was a magnificently unique time that forever transformed me and my life. If you ever have the opportunity to give of yourself in this manner, don't pass it up. While we sought for people to teach in Princeton, New Jersey, we came upon a doctoral student of philosophy. He was gracious and we had two wonderful discussions with him about the reality of God, and how he could possibly come to know with some degree of assurance that what we were telling him was true. He had some early family roots in Christianity but had long since moved toward agnosticism (neither claiming belief nor disbelief in God). He was a man of science and well acquainted with the scientific method and its emphasis on observation, experimentation, and measurement. I remember leaving his home after our first visit with an agreement that we would return, and that by then, he would have read a few passages of scripture, and sought God in prayer.

I recall returning to his home a couple of days later. He treated us with sincere kindness, and reported that he had read and prayed regarding the things we had discussed. As we asked him about his experience, he stated that he had figured something out. Our interest was obviously piqued, as he shared with us what he thought was the Lord's scientific method. It was brilliant! He had made a few small adaptations to the scientific method and had come up with a rudimentary divine method. It included experimentation (studying and living the Gospel), observation (noticing the fruits of living the Gospel), and then asking God. **Ultimately, a testimony or witness of divine truths is a gift of God, and can only be attained when we tap into that pipeline.** Much like when Jesus asked the disciples who the people thought He was, and they responded, "Some say that thou art John the Baptist: some, Elias;

and others, Jeremias, or one of the prophets." Jesus then asked the apostles themselves, "But whom say ye that I am? And Simon Peter answered and said, Thou art the Christ, the Son of the living God. And Jesus answered and said unto him, Blessed art thou, Simon Bar-jona: for flesh and blood hath not revealed it unto thee, but my Father which is in heaven."

We can utilize the Lord's scientific method to uncover the truth, and yet much like a swimmer who is looking to learn how to swim, we do not go to a boxer to gain swimming skills; instead, we must seek those who know of God and Christ and have felt of Their love and goodness.

Testimonies can be fragile. They are living things that are meant to stay relevant and fresh. Even a breathtaking sunrise or sunset can become commonplace and ultimately lose its appeal to the senses, if we don't take the time to take it in and appreciate it; likewise, we must mind-fully and deliberately keep our testimonies stunning and new. To do this we must keep rediscovering them. Perhaps Christ's wise invitation to be childlike included the wonderful curiosity and wonder that a child naturally experiences as she interacts with the world. I'm reminded of one of my favorite books, Antoine Saint-Exupery's *The Little Prince* (I love that story). One of my favorite quotes occurs when the little prince meets a very wise fox, who teaches him this valuable lesson: "And now here is my secret, a very simple secret: it is only with the heart that one can see rightly; what is essential is invisible to the eye."

My dear friend, experiment with the Gospel of Jesus Christ. Plant it in your heart. Clear the weeds, remove the rocks, and give that seed room to breathe and grow. I pray to God that you will do so and that, by and by, your Father who is Heaven will work a mighty miracle in you, and transform that small seed into a confident and fruitful tree.

LIFE HACK #66
PICK 3 SCRIPTURE PASSAGES THAT INSPIRE YOU & MEMORIZE THEM.

Chapter 67
The Christian Paradox

The depth and breadth of the Gospel is exciting. There is no end to the lessons and treasures that are found in it. I'm utterly fascinated by the teachings of the Savior. His teachings carry an amazing simplicity, but also require a lifetime of study. The great Christian paradox found in the Gospel of Matthew is such a principle:

"Then said Jesus unto his disciples, if any man will come after me, let him deny himself, and take up his cross, and follow me. For whosoever will save his life shall lose it, and whosoever will lose his life for my sake shall find it. For what is a man profited, if he shall gain the whole world, and lose his own soul? Or what shall a man give in exchange for his soul?"

The idea that we must lose ourselves and our lives for His sake, in order to find it (the Christian Paradox), is an idea worth pondering. The piercing questions that follow the Christian Paradox are of even greater worth. Think of them in a personal way: **What is the benefit of gaining the whole world, and yet losing your own soul? What am I willing to do and give in exchange for my soul?** Christ was constantly expanding the minds of His disciples. Christ's challenge and invitation to live in the world but not be of the world is another paradox that is of great significance.

In order to shed some light on these questions, and what they potentially mean to us, let me tell you the story of when Jesus met the Samaritan woman at the well. I will tell it in my own words:

While Jesus rested by Jacob's well, a Samaritan woman came to fetch some water.

Jesus asked her to draw him some water. She was surprised. No Jewish man would ever speak to a Samaritan woman. In addition, in those days, whatever a Samaritan touched would be pronounced unclean; thus, for Jesus to ask this woman to get him some water must have been surprising indeed. Jesus said, "If you knew the gift of God, and who it is that saith to thee, give me to drink, then you would have asked, and he would have given you living water." The woman was still unsure, and responded, "Sir, thou hast nothing to draw with, and the well is deep: from where do you have this living water that you speak of?" Jesus responded, "Whoever drinks of this water shall thirst again: but whoever drinks of the water that I shall give him shall never thirst; but the water that I shall give him shall be in him a well of water springing up into everlasting life." The wise woman said, "Sir, give me of this water that I thirst not."

What is this living water that He speaks of? It is the transformative and eternal Gospel of Jesus Christ. **Christ's loving desire to raise His disciples' vision above that of the world was a constant concern of His. More importantly perhaps is Jesus' desire to do the same with you.** To you He says, "These things I have spoken unto you, that in me ye might have peace. In the world ye shall have tribulation: but be of good cheer; I have overcome the world." I love His hopeful and encouraging words, "**Be of good cheer.**"

Keeping our minds and hearts looking upward is a constant challenge, especially because so much of our vision is kept entertained and engaged looking down. We are immersed in the world. We are constantly bathed in the ever-changing philosophies of men. Our phones constantly invade our senses with a steady stream of "the world," and divert our efforts away from what is of great worth, and toward much that is meaningless. We must manage our phones, or they will easily manage us. **Our phones can be an amazing source of connection and interaction, and yet more and more research suggests that the more time we spend "connecting" via our phones, the more lonely and disconnected we feel. How can that be possible? Think of it like eating popcorn. We can fill our bodies full of the stuff to the point that we "feel" full, yet there is nothing of substance in us, and all that we are left with is a bunch of popcorn kernels stuck in our teeth, and a film of**

butter coating our teeth. **Such are the draw and wages of the world. We can fill our lives with worldly pursuits that, interestingly enough, leave us empty and constantly obsessing about having more**.

My gentle suggestion for you is this: Connect heavenward for 10 to 20 minutes or more on a daily basis. Raise your standard a bit! Instead of closing out your day with Instagram and Facebook, do it with scripture study and deliberate prayer. Begin your day with prayer, meditation, exercise, and connecting with your family and siblings, instead of connecting to media. **Be where you are!** You know what I'm saying? Connect to the things that are within your physical reach first, and second to those that are far away. **Teach your brain to seek for the things of greater worth, and that will yield the greatest and richest gain, instead of training your brain to be enslaved by the prompts and notices of your phones**. Please don't be offended. I promise I'm not trying to be just one more adult telling you how bad phones can be. I get you! I'm with you! Just use yours wisely, and turn your attention toward those things that truly promote joy, and not just entertainment.

What will you give in exchange for your soul? What will you add? What will you subtract? What are you not doing that you should? What are you doing that you shouldn't? Write three quick goals for yourself that will improve your divine connection, then create a simple plan and reminder to make it happen. Love ya!

Goal 1: _____

Goal 2: _____

Goal 3: _____

LIFE HACK #67
"HE WHO IS NOT A GOOD SERVANT WILL NOT BE A GOOD MASTER."
-PLATO

CHAPTER 68
THE PRODIGAL

There are few parables that speak to our hearts more than the parable of the prodigal son. This parable is also known as the parable of the two lost sons (you'll see why in just a few moments). It's a story about redemption, and **redemption is something we all desperately need and that our soul desires.** It's really a story about becoming lost, coming to oneself, and being found. The story is set as Jesus calls and begins to teach publicans and sinners. As He begins to do this, He is criticized by the Pharisees and Sadducees, because he keeps company with sinners. Jesus in His usual style, challenges the doctrine and myopic thinking of the Pharisees by revealing to them the love that God is for all of His children, and how the heavens rejoice over every soul that is redeemed and ultimately returns to God. Behold, the parable of the prodigal son:

> "A certain man had two sons: And the younger of them said to his father, Father, give me the portion of goods that falleth to me. And he divided unto them his living. And not many days the younger son gathered all together, and took his journey into a far country, and there wasted his substance with riotous living. And when he had spent all, there arose a mighty famine in that land; and he began to be in want. And he went and joined himself to a citizen of that country; and he sent him into his fields to feed swine. And he would fain have filled his belly with the husks that the swine did eat: and no man gave unto him.
> And when he came to himself, he said, How many hired servants of my father's have bread enough and to spare, and I perish with hunger! I will arise and go to my father, and will say unto him, Father, I have sinned against heaven, and before thee, and am no more worthy to be called thy son: make me as one of thy hired servants.

And he arose, and came to his father. But when he was yet a great way off, his father saw him, and had compassion, and ran, and fell on his neck, and kissed him. And the son said unto him, Father, I have sinned against heaven, and in thy sight, and am no more worthy to be called thy son. But the father said to his servants, bring forth the best robe, and put it on him; and put a ring on his hand, and shoes on his feet: and bring hither the fatted calf, and kill it; and let us eat, and be merry: for this my son was dead, and is alive again; he was lost, and is found. And they began to be merry.

Now his elder son was in the field: and as he came and drew nigh to the house, he heard music and dancing. And he called one of the servants, and asked what these things meant. And he said unto him, thy brother is come; and thy father hath killed the fatted calf, because he hath received him safe and sound. And he was angry, and would not go in: therefore came his father out, and entreated him. And he answering said to his father, Lo, these many years do I serve thee, neither transgressed I at any time thy commandment: and yet thou never gavest me a kid, that I might make merry with my friends: but as soon as this thy son was come, which hath devoured thy living with harlots, thou hast killed for him the fatted calf. And he said unto him, Son, thou art ever with me, and all that I have is thine. It was meet that we should make merry, and be glad: for this thy brother was dead, and is alive again; and was lost, and is found."

I just love that parable. There is so much that we can go into, so much to expound and ponder about. Can I share with you my favorite parts?

- **God and the church are soft places to land:** I love how the father (who is a representation of God) saw him "when he was yet a great way off," which to me means that God the Father is watching and waiting for His sons and daughters to return to Him. In addition, it teaches me that when we begin to make even the smallest of changes (still a great way off), He comes to get us and brings us back into His presence. I love how the Father kisses his son, puts his best robe around his shoulders, puts a ring in his hand, and shoes on his feet. I love that he throws a party! Isn't it marvelous that a loving God is just a prayer away?

- **Don't keep score and let bitterness contaminate you:** Did you catch why this is also called the parable of the two lost sons? During the story, the older son hears about the party that is going on and finds out that his father has killed the fatted calf and is celebrating with his son who has been up to no good. He becomes filled with indignation and resentment, and as a result becomes lost himself. He refuses to go into the party. Here again, this kind and loving father goes out to him, listens to him, teaches him, and then gently encourages him to return and celebrate.

- **If you find yourself in the desert:** Sometimes we make ignorant choices in our lives. We unconsciously and insecurely choose paths that appear harmless, and yet days, months, and years later we find ourselves in the desert, suffering, disconnected, bitter, without purpose or direction. If you find yourself in the middle of the Sahara, it's time to 'come to yourself' just as the prodigal did, and return. Did you catch his change of heart? He wasn't just returning, he was coming back to apologize and to be a servant. There was precious humility in this man, and that is what ultimately helped him "come to himself." So, if you find yourself in your own personal desert of affliction, don't blame others, don't be afraid or too proud to ask for help—instead, begin to take some steps in a new direction and, little by little, you'll find yourself in a new and better place.

- **The seeds of redemption:** Every mistake you make in life contains in it the seeds of redemption. Christ didn't just pay the price for our mistakes, He forever changed what mistakes mean. The Atonement (His sacrifice), allows for our most scandalous behavior and our most obnoxious weaknesses to become strengths unto us. This doesn't justify our stupidity, but it does allow us to return to Him and to receive the best that He has to give us.

- **The wages of sin:** Should you find yourself in a strange land, hungry, alone, wishing to fill your belly with the cornhusks you would feed a swine, remember that your best thinking brought you here. It's of critical importance that you see your role in how you arrived here, because if you brought yourself here, then you can certainly take yourself out! I'm reminded of this awesome quote by C.S. Lewis in his amazing little book called *The Screwtape Letters*: *"It does not matter how small the sins are provided that their cumulative effect is to edge the man away from the Light and out into the Nothing. Murder is no better than cards if cards can do the trick. Indeed the safest road to Hell is the gradual one—the gentle slope, soft underfoot, without sudden turnings, without milestones, without signposts."* Stand in holy places, with holy people, doing holy things. Ultimately, you will become holy yourself and then you can go and strengthen those around you.

I hope you have come to admire this powerful story as I do. It contains so much goodness and so much wisdom. Read it, study it, and see which parts stick out to you the very most. **For me the most beautiful part of the story is the glimpse it gives us into the character of God**. I just love how He (represented by the father) treats both of the sons. I love the father's words to the oldest son who fell into bitterness: *"Son, thou art ever with me, and all that I have is thine."* I've found that the most important knowledge that we can attain in this life is that there is a Father and a Mother in Heaven, and that They love us. They are concerned, watching for us, and within our reach. **We must choose God—that is the deal! He will not force us, manipulate us, or guilt us into returning to Him. I believe that ultimately we will end up where we desire to be**. C.S. Lewis, in *The Great Divorce*, suggests that "There are only two kinds of people in the end: those who say to God, 'Thy will be done,' and those to whom God says, in the end, 'Thy will be done.' All that are in Hell, choose it. Without that self-choice there could be no Hell. No soul that seriously and constantly desires joy will ever miss it. Those who seek find. Those who knock it is opened." His invitation to "come and see," and to "follow thou me," is in full swing. As your friend, I truly hope that you will seek for that Christ who stands open-armed to receive you. Love you.

Life Hack #68

"A great man is always willing to be little."
-Ralph Waldo Emerson

CHAPTER 69
3 LESSONS I LEARNED FROM PETER

I enjoy Peter. We don't know a lot about him, and yet what we do know allow us to have some idea about who he was, as well as his strengths and weaknesses. There is much to say about Peter, but there are four events that I just absolutely love and that can teach us some valuable things. I've already shared one (Chapter 19: People, Places, and Things), so I'll tell you about the other three:

- **Walking on water:** Jesus had separated himself from the apostles to go pray. During that time, the apostles took to the sea, likely to do some fishing, and were caught up in a storm during the night. While in the storm Jesus came to them, walking on the water. The apostles were frightened, but their fears were relieved when they heard the voice of the Master saying, *"Be of good cheer; it is I; be not afraid."* Upon hearing this, Peter said, *"Lord, if it be thou, bid me come unto thee on the water. And he said, Come. And when Peter was come down out of the ship, he walked on the water, to go to Jesus. But when he saw the wind boisterous, he was afraid; and beginning to sink, he cried, saying, Lord, save me. And immediately Jesus stretched forth his hand, and caught him, and said unto him, O thou of little faith, wherefore didst thou doubt?"* I love Peter's desire to come unto Christ, and to try walking on the water. It appears that he was successful for a moment, but then he began to notice the wind and the waves, and began to sink. **The powerful lesson here is that faith follows focus. It is the difference between walking on water, and focusing on the water (instead of focusing on Christ).** There is power in Christ. There is power in following Him, learning to be like Him, and in studying about Him. Miracles can attend us when we seek Him and trust Him with our lives.

- **Jump naked:** After the Savior died and had appeared the to the apostles several times, he once again appeared unto them while they were at sea fishing. This time the Apostles had had no luck, and caught no fish. Jesus watched them and called out to them from the shore, *"Children have ye any meat? They answered him, no. And he said unto them, Cast the net on the right side of the ship, and ye shall find. They cast therefore, and now they were not able to draw it for the multitude of fishes. Therefore that disciple whom Jesus loved saith unto Peter, It is the Lord. Now when Simon Peter heard that it was the Lord, he girt his fisher's coat unto him, (for he was naked,) and did cast himself into the sea."* I love Peter's sincere and impulsive desire to be by the Savior. **No clothes...no problem!** I believe Peter truly loved the Savior, and wanted to be near Him. **Remember that we are meant to have a relationship with our Heavenly Father and His Son.** That means, time, effort, and focus. Draw near unto Him, and He will draw near unto you...and, oh yeah, you can keep your clothes on while you go to Him!

- **Feed my sheep:** Continuing with the aforementioned event where Peter dove into the sea to be with the Savior, the remainder of the apostles brought the boat to shore with the fish they had caught. Jesus was prepared for them with a fire, and fish cooking on it. While with the Peter, the Lord asked him three piercing questions: *"Simon, son of Jonas, lovest thou me more than these? He saith unto him, Yea, Lord; thou knowest that I love thee. He saith unto him, Feed my lambs. He saith to him again the second time, Simon, son of Jonas, lovest thou me? He saith unto him, Yea, Lord; thou knowest that I love thee. He saith unto him, Feed my sheep. He saith unto him the third time, Simon, son of Jonas, lovest thou me? Peter was grieved because he said unto him the third time, Lovest thou me? And he said unto him, Lord, thou knowest all things; thou knowest that I love thee. Jesus saith unto him, Feed my sheep."* I believe that after the death of the Savior, the apostles may have been a little lost, fearful, and discouraged, so much so that they went back to being regular fishermen. The Lord's questioning of Peter was an attempt to re-focus him. Jeffrey R. Holland (a modern-day apostle) wrote about this very moment: *"Then Peter, why are you here? Why are we back on this same shore, by these same nets, having this same conversation? Wasn't it obvious then and isn't it obvious now that if I want fish, I can get fish? What I need, Peter, are disciples—and I need them forever. I need someone to feed my sheep and save my lambs. I need someone to preach my gospel and defend my faith."* **Jesus calls us with the same high calling. He beckons us to join Him not as fishers of fish, but as fishers of humankind. What the Savior needs are disciples traveling the path of discipleship.** Imagine Jesus questioning you in the very same manner. Peter did answer the call, and did go and struggle and strive to establish Christ's church and preach His gospel, until He was crucified upside down in Rome.

LIFE HACK #69

"THE PAST IS BEHIND, LEARN FROM IT. THE FUTURE IS AHEAD,
PREPARE FOR IT. THE PRESENT IS HERE, LIVE IT."
- THOMAS S. MONSON

Chapter 70
You Are that You Might Have Joy

If your psychology (the way you think and perceive the world around you) is everything, then the Gospel of Jesus Christ is the ultimate psychology—it is the ultimate lens. Lehi, an ancient prophet who lived in the Americas, stated the following before he died: "Adam fell that man might be, and men are that they might have joy." **As you seek for joy in your life, remember that joy is an outcome—it is a realization of certain truths about ourselves and the world around us, paired with our acting upon those truths**. What are those life-changing truths?

- **Nothing can or will separate you from the love of God:** The Apostle Paul taught the Romans, "For I am persuaded, that neither death, nor life, nor angels, nor principalities, nor powers, nor things present, nor things to come, nor height, nor depth, nor any other creature, shall be able to separate us from the love of God, which is in Christ Jesus our Lord." This speaks to me and teaches a powerful doctrine that **no matter what stupidity or ignorance I act out in my life, I somehow never travel beyond the love and radical loyalty that God and Jesus Christ have for me. I'm always worthy of returning and reforming**. This is a powerful hope that can light your whole being. Your hope in the correct things is a major factor in whether you experience joy or not in your life. **If your level of hope is higher than your level of despair and discouragement, then happiness follows, simply because the brain and body believe that your moments of struggle will not only pass, but they too will become part of the divine tapestry that your life will become**. God loves you. He believes in you. He is fiercely loyal to you and will always receive you in your sincerity. Seek Him, for His "yoke is easy, and [His] burden is light," and as you find Him here and there, may His joy, love, and hope fill your cup.

- **God is the most joyous being in the universe:** Your life is no cosmic accident. God has a plan, and included in that plan of happiness is our travail here on this lovely planet, and our joyful return into His presence to live the same quality of life that He lives. That is the deal. That is what He has in store for us—a full and complete inheritance of all that He has. **God is not looking for slaves, nor is He looking for brainwashed disciples. He is looking for people who will heed the invitation to follow Him, and as they do, they will worship Him, not because they must, but because His goodness, love, and mercy make Him a being worthy of worship. God's hope is greater than the world's despair.** Hang in there through your times of difficulty. Self-help is powerful, but seeking divine help and understanding divine truth is ultimately more powerful.

- **Every experience can be consecrated:** Realizing that every life experience, every event, accident, or circumstance can be had for our good and experience, is possibly the most hopeful and peacemaking doctrine I know of. **All things can be consecrated for our good. To consecrate means to make holy or to purify. You are a part of God's plan. He has not forgotten about you. The suffering, abuse, unfairness, grief, and disappointments that you have and will suffer, can be transformed by the Atonement of Jesus Christ into beautiful light and power.** It is true! This concept is not psychological fluff or me blowing hot air. It is real, and with God's help **we are able to transform and synthesize any negative event into a strength.** The words of the prophet Moroni are ringing in my ear this very moment, reminding me that "if men come unto me I will show unto them their weakness. I give unto men weakness that they may be humble; and my grace is sufficient for all men that humble themselves before me; for if they humble themselves before me, and have faith in me, then will I make weak things become strong unto them." Know that this true, and know that God stands with you. **We are never truly lost as long as the Master of the Universe and His Beloved Son are in our corner—and They are always in our corner!**

- **We are agents unto ourselves:** Our ability to choose for ourselves is a critical part of our experience here on earth. Think of freedom and agency on a continuum. **We are learning to be free.** We are experimenting with the idea of being agents unto ourselves. As we seek and gather more knowledge, our ability to become wise choosers increases. Mistakes, errors in judgment, and pure stupidity are our lot in life, in part because we are ignorant. **We are all fools, but we are learning fools. As you lean into the Gospel of Jesus Christ, eternal truth will slowly make its way into your very soul. As this happens the most amazing transformation will take place. You will become a new man or woman.** You will become the physical manifestation of "the light and the salt of the earth." You will go from natural to spiritual, and then you too will overcome the world, and your focus will be closer to God's focus and purpose. Now go and choose wisely.

- **In the end, all will be made right:** Lynn G. Robbins stated that "Repentance isn't [God's] backup plan in the event we might fail. Repentance is His plan, knowing that we will." I believe that Christ can heal our earthly infirmities, but if not (and this is very important information), He can help to shape our backs so that we may carry the burden. I've known individuals who seemingly carry the weight of the world on their backs. They have suffered tragically in their lives, and live afflicted lives. I feel for them. Life is a daily, even hourly, struggle for them. I pray and hope that the

Savior can help them. I also realize that you and I are part of the great army that can help them. **Discipleship is about aligning with God and becoming His hands in mortality.** Let us become strong so that we can strengthen those around us. God needs you and me! **Let us become healers of humankind, and by doing so, heal ourselves.**

My wonderful friend I am a believer! I'm happy to say it—more importantly, I'm grateful to be able to say it. **I hope you know that Christ and the Gospel of Jesus Christ are the safest and softest places to land in this world.** His arms are outstretched to receive you regardless of what you have done or gone through. I love you and have great aspirations and hope for you. Do great and be great. Be kind and understanding of others. Remember that heeding the call from Savior of the world is a personal choice. You cannot be forced, cajoled, guilted, or shamed into being a disciple of Christ. Teach gently, invite sincerely, and love wholeheartedly. May God be with you 'til we meet again.

LIFE HACK #70
CREATE A RUNNING LIST OF AWESOME QUOTES ON YOUR PHONE.

A Few Parting Words...

My wonderful friend, I smile just knowing that you are there. I hope you know that I'm cheering for you. I hope you have friends and family that love you. **I hope you know that you are a walking miracle, and that your brain and body are made to grow and evolve.** There is nothing merely normal or average about you. Your capacity and potential are almost infinite (wow!). Don't throw your gift away! **Use your mind and your body in the most wonderful ways.** No matter the outcome, do not allow yourself to be trapped in your room, isolated from others, and caught up in some virtual reality. **The world awaits you and needs your brilliance.** Do not throw away your shot!

Be flexible! Be open to new experiences. Do not allow yourself to become rigid, stubborn, and unteachable, assuming that all that you have experienced in your short life defines you in some permanent way. **Give yourself time and room to grow and learn new things.** Never stop seeking, never cease knocking, and you will most certainly find the greatest that life has to offer. Remember that the ship of life ain't coming in—you have to swim out to get it. Jump in! **Stop waiting for people to do things, or for this or that to happen until you are happy—rise up and get out of that waiting place.** Don't allow mistakes and failures to discourage you from trying again and again. Remember Churchill's words: "Success is not final, failure is not fatal: it is the courage to continue that counts." I love you, I care for you, I respect you. Your mistakes won't ever define you, but also remember that your brain will create a shortcut for everything you repeatedly do. **Be wise. Be brave and grab hold of every good thing.** Let go of every faulty and limiting ideology that makes you insecure, lazy, isolated, and keeps you from trying new things or things that you don't think you're good at. Remember the power of "YET": "I'm not good at school...yet"; "I'm not good at sports...yet"; "I'm not a good friend...yet."

Remember that you are a meaning-making machine. Take control of what things mean to you. Don't allow your fearful and insecure brain to make all of your decisions. It's time to become more mind-full. It's time for you to chart a basic and dynamic course, so that you don't end up in the middle of the Sahara desert saying, "What the...?" **Be a little more attentive about where you place your feet. Become more aware of the things that go into your brain and that come out of your mouth. Remember, you are the one that manages that flow.** Do not allow any gossip to come out of your mouth, unless it is positive gossip.

You are gifted! Do not hide your gifts—show them to the world. **Bring your "A" game more often, and to more circumstances**. Work hard to be at your best at home with your mother, father, siblings, or whoever else constitutes your family. Listen, work your little tail off to make those relationships work— they carry so much importance and weight. If you can't do that, then connect yourself to people who are encouraging, inspiring, and who carry goodness with them wherever they go. More importantly, become that individual. **Don't let the injustices of life take you over to the dark side, where bitterness, anger, and unintelligent rebelliousness awaits. Whatever benefit you think will come from being there is a facade and will only cripple you and limit your choices.**

I so wish for your joy, and yet I know that, for some of you at least, happiness is not a constant or even frequent companion. If you find yourself frequently sad, low and unmotivated; and if you are avoiding things that are intelligent and potentially good because you are afraid or anxious, it's probably time for you to talk to a parent or adult that can help. We are out there for you, you know? To avoid help because you don't want to sound weak or because it will ruin your bravado is not a quality choice.

Make your life rich! Fill it with the best books, the best activities, the best friends, the best knowledge, the best talents, the best music. Take the riches of the world, and make them yours. Avoid all trash, smut, and media that degrades or exploits people. Manage your inputs! Life is beautiful—make sure you are out there to capture it and admire it. Find the most picturesque places where you live, and make sure you go there often. There is magic in the hills—there is strength and peace in nature to be had. Get out there! Camp, hike, climb, bike, swim, ski, snowboard, surf, fly a kite, rollerblade, walk, play sports, play games, run, but whatever you do, get out there more often...no excuses!

I love you. May God be with you wherever you go. **May He draw near to you, as you draw near to him. I hope that as you seek Him, He will reveal himself and His love to you. Be patient. I know you want it all at once, but all at once is not how things usually come.** Be steady and have some endurance, for heaven's sake! I'm done! That's all I got. Know that you've got a friend and supporter in me. Now get out there and Carpe Diem.

Your loyal friend,
Iuri Tiago Melo

Made in the USA
Columbia, SC
05 June 2019